Emotionally Intelligent Parenting

EMOTIONALLY

INTELLIGENT

PARENTING

■ ■ ■

How to Raise a Self-Disciplined,
Responsible, Socially Skilled Child

■ ■ ■

Maurice J. Elias, Ph.D.,
Steven E. Tobias, Psy.D., and
Brian S. Friedlander, Ph.D.

Foreword by Daniel Goleman

Three Rivers Press
New York

Published by Three Rivers Press,
201 East 50th Street, New York, New York 10022.
Member of the Crown Publishing Group.

Originally published in hardcover by Harmony Books, 1999.

Random House, Inc. New York, Toronto, London, Sydney, Auckland
www.randomhouse.com

Three Rivers Press is a registered trademark of Random House, Inc.

Printed in the United States of America

Design by Debbie Glasserman Design

Library of Congress Cataloging-in-Publication Data
Elias, Maurice J.
Emotionally intelligent parenting: how to raise a self-
disciplined, responsible, socially skilled child / by Maurice J.
Elias, Steven E. Tobias, and Brian S. Friedlander; foreword by
Daniel Goleman.
1. Child rearing.   2. Parenting.   I. Tobias, Steven E.
II. Friedlander, Brian S.   III. Title.
HQ769.E552   1999
649'.1—dc21   98-20835
CIP

ISBN 0-609-80483-9

10 9 8 7 6 5 4 3 2 1

First Paperback Edition

To my children, Sara Elizabeth and Samara Alexandra. You have taught me a great deal about parenting and about children, and you enrich my life beyond what I can ever put into words.

MJE

To my children, Meg and Gillian, and to your generation. I try to be emotionally intelligent and to teach these skills to others so that the world you and your peers inherit will be safe, your relationships gratifying, and your lives fulfilling.

SET

In loving memory to my mother, Marilyn Friedlander, who taught me the importance of unconditional love, family, and learning. Even in your absence, you still continue to inspire me to new heights.

BSF

Acknowledgments

■　■　■

I thank my family for putting up with the disruptions that my writing creates in our lives and in our living room and dining room. My wife, Ellen, has been my partner in parenting and in just about everything else for over 348 annimontharies, and her unwavering support keeps me moving forward. I also want to thank my professional colleagues at the Collaborative for the Advancement of Social and Emotional Learning (CASEL), with whom I continue to work to apply the principles of emotional intelligence to education; the hard-working and dedicated members of the Social Problem Solving Unit at UMDNJ; the fabulous teachers of emotional intelligence at flagship schools in Highland Park, Piscataway, Berkeley Heights, and Cape May Courthouse, New Jersey; the Children's Institute in Verona, New Jersey, and Kiryat Ono in the Tel Aviv metropolitan school district; the graduate and undergraduate students at Rutgers whom I have had the privilege to teach and supervise over the past two decades; and four very special colleagues with whom I hope to continue working for many more years to come: Ed Dunkelblau, Tom Schuyler, Linda Bruene-Butler, and Bernie Novick. Each of these individuals is a lifelong friend whose dedication to children and to reaching people in a genuine and engaging way has set standards that I continue to strive to meet.

MJE

I would like to thank all of my teachers for making this book possible. From Miss Pazulli in kindergarten to Dr. Marvin Bram in college, and all the stimulating and caring teachers in between, I gratefully acknowledge your contribution to my personal and academic development. My wife, Carol, has also been my teacher, cheerleader, and friend whose support has enabled me to achieve my goals. I truly appreciate her. In listing my teachers, I also include my parents, Ruth Zitt, Hersch Zitt, and George Tobias, who taught me ideals and problem solving; my sister Susan, who is my friend; my colleagues, from whom I have learned both professionally and personally; and my clients, who not only show their confidence in me but who also continually give me new ideas and teach me compassion.

SET

Through all the countless hours spent working on this project and many others, my wife, Helene, has been a continual source of encouragement and support. Without her, these projects would seem insurmountable. Likewise, I would like to acknowledge my daughter, Chelsea, who has provided me with a rich palette of parenting experiences to draw from. I would also like to thank my father, Robert Friedlander, who has always given me a strong model and basis for Emotionally Intelligent Parenting. To my in-laws, Hyman and Ruth Gorelick, thanks for all your love and support. Also to my brother-in-law Victor and sister-in-law Kathie, thanks for your excitement and enthusiasm. And I would like to thank my brother, Devin, and sister-in-law, Sara, and my sister Susan and brother-in-law, David, and their families for all their support and encouragement and for believing in me.

BSF

We have many colleagues, and friends, and relatives whose support and inspiration have allowed us to pursue this work. Among these, we want to thank especially Dan Goleman, whose great insights and skills as a communicator have opened up the area of social and emotional intelligence to millions of individuals throughout the world and who supported us in our application of this work to parents. We also thank a special set of colleagues at the Center for Applied Psychology of the Graduate School of Applied and Professional Psychology at Rutgers University. Dr. Lew Gantwerk and Diane Crino have given us forums to conduct workshops and other kinds of outreach that have allowed us to perfect our messages and solidify many of our understandings. We expect to continue to work with them for many years. We also want to thank Denise Marcil, our literary agent, for her confidence in us, her patience, her creativity, and her energy. She has taught us a great deal about what it means to be authors. Thanks also to all of Denise's assistants, who have helped us manage many logistical issues. Finally, our thanks to Peter Guzzardi, senior editor at Harmony Books, who truly loves kids, wants to help them manage in these difficult times, and knows so much about writing. Peter also has helped us work with a wonderfully talented group of professionals at Harmony in editing, marketing, and sales, both in the United States and overseas. Without this team, our book would not have reached so many parents and other caregivers so effectively. And that is our goal—helping those who care for children to do so in an emotionally intelligent manner.

Family life is our first school for emotional learning: in this intimate cauldron we learn how to feel about ourselves and how others will react to our feelings; how to think about these feelings and what choices we have in reacting; how to read and express hopes and fears. This emotional school operates not just through the things that parents say and do directly to children, but also in the models they offer for handling their own feelings and those that pass between husband and wife.

DANIEL GOLEMAN

Contents

■   ■   ■

9. The Emotionally Intelligent Parenting Doctors Are In: Sound EQ Parenting Bites to Help with Common Family Issues 218

Foreword
by Daniel Goleman

■   ■   ■

If there was ever a time when parents needed the kind of guidance offered in *Emotionally Intelligent Parenting*, it is now.

As a parent, I'm particularly troubled by data from a nationwide random survey in which American children, seven to fourteen years old, were rated by their parents and teachers—adults who know them well. Done first in the mid 1970s, then repeated with a similar cohort in the late 1980s, the survey found that, on average, America's children declined across the board on basic indicators of emotional intelligence.

They were more impulsive and disobedient, more anxious and fearful, more lonely and sad, more irritable and violent. In short, children declined on forty-two such indicators and improved on none—a very strong trend. Simultaneously over those years, there were abrupt jumps in the rates of teen violence, suicide, and rape. Most chilling to me is the growing number of weapons-related killings in our schools.

Why this erosion of the basic capacities for living? I believe that children are the unintended victims of two forces at large on the world stage, one economic, the other technological. The ratcheting up of global competitiveness means that today's generation of parents has to work longer and harder to maintain a decent standard of living than was true for their own parents' generation—it's not that we love our children less, but we have less free time to spend with them than our own parents did with us.

At the same time, increased mobility for families means that fewer and fewer have relatives like a grandmother in the neighborhood to take up the slack. All too many families live in neighborhoods where they are afraid to let their younger children play outside unsupervised—let alone go into a neighbor's home.

On the technological side, there is an unprecedented experiment going on with the world's youth: more children than ever before in human history are spending more hours of their lives than ever staring at a video monitor. Whether they are absorbed in an educational CD-ROM or watching junk TV, the fact is, they are not out playing with other children.

The way we've passed on the basic skills of emotional intelligence from generation to generation is in life—in playing with other kids, and from our parents, relatives, and neighbors. Childhood has changed: children no longer have the natural opportunities for this kind of learning than was true throughout our history.

And that suggests the need of every parent to do the very best job we can in helping our children master these most basic skills in life. We are our children's main tutors in this realm. It is in the small, everyday interactions of parent and child that these lessons are learned. *Emotionally Intelligent Parenting* is about those everyday interactions. It is about using a powerful method called "Keep Calm" when, as a parent, you are upset, as well as to help cool off your children's anger. It is about understanding and respecting the feelings of family members in these hectic times, with many ideas to reduce household stress and increase the time parents and children spend laughing together. One feature of *Emotionally Intelligent Parenting* that will help many parents immediately is the Parenting "Sound Bites"—quick, practical ideas for handling everyday routines in an emotionally intelligent manner, from waking up to bedtime and many points in between, for preschoolers and teenagers alike.

I should also like to add that I have worked with Maurice Elias and I can say he is an authoritative, caring source of advice for parents.

To be sure, Dr. Spock's words of advice to parents hold true: "you know more than you think you do" about parenting. But any parent—and any child—will benefit from heeding the very practical, well-tested, and sound guidelines offered here. I think Dr. Spock would have appreciated *Emotionally Intelligent Parenting*. I know I do.

Emotionally Intelligent Parenting

Chapter 1

The Twenty-four-Karat Golden Rule: Why It Is Important to Build Self-Discipline, Responsibility, and Emotional Health in Children

■ ■ ■

Do you know the Golden Rule? Most people do. Usually, it is quoted, "Do unto others as you would have others do unto you." We call this "the Fourteen-Karat Golden Rule." Why? Because there is a better one, one that reflects what we call Emotionally Intelligent Parenting:

Do unto your children as you would have other people do unto your children.

We insist that others honor and respect our children, talk to them with courtesy and consideration, and not physically hurt them. How have you reacted when someone has dishonored your children in some way? Perhaps it was a teacher, or someone in a store, or the parent of another child. We are sure you were upset and asked, among other things, what they thought they were doing and how dare they do that. Yet a moment of honest reflection might reveal times when we have said and done things to our own children for which, if an outsider tried them, we would want them arrested and imprisoned.

The difference between the Fourteen- and Twenty-four-Karat Golden Rules is Emotionally Intelligent Parenting. The Twenty-four-Karat Rule requires us to know our feelings well, to take our child's perspective with empathy, to control our own impulses, to monitor carefully what we are doing as parents, to work in a dedicated way to improve our parenting, and to use social skill in carrying out ideas.

The Fourteen-Karat Rule is not strong enough to serve as a guide for parenting now. Times have changed. Life is hectic, complicated, exciting, challenging, and exhausting. We have ever-increasing information overload. The time is right for a new Golden Rule for parenting. We haven't had one since Benjamin Spock and Haim Ginott came on the scene—over three decades ago. It's time for a new paradigm for parenting, for a new century and millennium: Emotionally Intelligent Parenting.

What can Emotionally Intelligent Parenting do for your household? First, it will help bring about more peace with less stress. It is a way to restore a sense of balance when stress takes its toll and the kids start fighting, cooperation turns to conflict, your teenagers rebel, and members of the family get frustrated with everything that seems to need to be done immediately. Some stress can be motivating, but too much keeps us from being at our best. It is difficult for individuals under stress to do what, in calmer circumstances, they know is right.

It's a Difficult Time to Be a Parent—or a Child

This is a very demanding time during which to be a parent. Maybe the only thing more difficult is to be a child. There are more influences than ever on children, and more sources of distraction. James Comer—a professor of child psychiatry at the Yale Child Study Center and the author of the books *School Power* and *Waiting for a Miracle: Schools Can't Solve Our Problems, But We Can*, and a leader in addressing the concerns of all youth, especially those in our urban centers—pointed out in a 1997 interview that never before in human history has there been so much information going directly to children that is unfiltered by adult caregivers. Cornell University child development specialist Uri

Bronfenbrenner observed that we are in the age of hectic activity; we are busy planning how to get our kids to where they have to be next, to get ourselves where we have to be, rushing from one thing to another, wondering if all of our arrangements will work out. Put this all together and you have a parenting situation with all the calmness and order of the inside of a blender making a mixed fruit drink.

There is a profusion of parenting fads. And just about every idea that comes along gets cloned, usually without authenticity or any hope of delivering on promises made. The stress does not seem to diminish. Parents do not know where to turn. What we must not lose sight of, however, is that the basics of human biology, child rearing, and parent-child relationships have not changed. Daniel Goleman's international best-seller, *Emotional Intelligence*, makes the point that we have neglected the biology of our feelings as adults and as parents, and we have neglected the role of feelings in our children's healthy growth. We are now paying the price, as families and as a society, with a higher incidence of violence and disrespectful behavior. We are paying for it when we see seemingly sensible teenagers becoming parents, then getting rid of newborns as if they were unwanted supermarket purchases. We are paying when we emphasize the intellect of students but forget their hearts. And of course, our children pay as well, as their unhappiness and troubled behaviors continue to grow.

LET'S BRING EMOTIONAL INTELLIGENCE
TO EVERYDAY PARENTING

This book picks up where Daniel Goleman's book leaves off. In it, we intend to help parents understand why emotional intelligence is so important to the task of everyday parenting and creating household peace and harmony. We do this with authenticity, having worked with Daniel Goleman. In fact, the theory of emotional intelligence is based on decades of research and professional practice, including our own. In addition, as parents, we understand what parents go through. We know that Emotionally Intelligent Parenting must respect everyday parenting pressures and deal realistically with time. Parents' time is extremely valuable; they cannot afford to lose time and emotional energy to household turmoil, poor relationships with their kids, or kids who are out of control and lack responsibility, self-discipline, and the ability to separate what is genuinely in their interest from values dictated by peer pressure and the media.

Emotionally Intelligent Parenting uses specific, simple, important techniques that can make a major contribution to household peace and harmony. All these techniques have been developed from the authors' hands-on work with parents, families, and schools. The concept is founded on parents working with their own and their children's emotions in intelligent, constructive, positive, creative ways, respecting biological realities and the role of feelings in human nature. It draws its strength from small changes, repeated day after day, in our relationships with our children. Emotionally Intelligent Parenting is both a new paradigm for parenting and a highly realistic and practical approach to it. And a big part of Emotionally Intelligent Parenting is to remove a little stress and bring more fun into our families and our relationships with our children.

WE ARE NOT TALKING ABOUT BAD PARENTS OR BAD KIDS

Some children are born with particularly difficult temperaments, while other children seem to acquire them through painful experiences in life. It is important to keep in mind that children do not want to be bad. A bad child is not happy, no matter how it may seem to the parents and others. A child who misbehaves is seeking, though unsuccessfully, to learn ways to be viable in the world, which means to learn self-discipline, responsibility, and social and emotional intelligence.

In this book we will not be talking about "bad" parents or "bad" kids, nor will we ever suggest that you should feel guilt for being an inadequate parent, or blame your spouse or society or the child. Instead, we plan to teach you how to build concrete skills. Learning new parenting skills and teaching new emotional and social skills to your child—the skills of emotional intelligence—can be exciting, because it can improve the quality of life in your household and better prepare your children for the future. And, even though we are not blaming anyone, we are placing the responsibility for doing something about it on parents. To be a parent means to take responsibility for acting as a household leader, for helping children grow up to be emotionally intelligent. It is up to parents to use and to teach the skills that will enable children to achieve the goals parents have set for them.

Is This You?

As a way of starting to look at how to make family life more harmonious and beneficial for children, we would like you to take a look at the following common family events, to see if one or more of them sounds familiar to you:

1. Your preschooler is supposed to be getting dressed, but he is distracted by toys in the room, clouds in the sky, molecules of air...whatever. You need to get to work on time.

2. Your elementary-school child gets home from school at three o'clock. Sports practice starts at three-thirty. But religious instruction starts at four on certain days. And then there is that project with a couple of other kids that needs to be done. Your child has lost the schedule of when all these things are taking place. It is 3:10 P.M. on Thursday, and you are not sure where

you are supposed to be, or when you are to be there, or who is driving.

3. Your middle-school child is getting ready for the seventh-grade dance. But you said her room had to be cleaned, things hung up and put away, and homework done before she could go. Although she assured you that all this was done, you see that it is far from done and that it cannot be done in the time remaining. Car pools have been arranged, you have plans for the evening, and she is just about dressed and ready, although her phone is still stuck to her ear. You are not sure what to do, and you feel a strong need to sit down.

4. Ah, high school. There is a student congress meeting at 7:00 A.M. Chorus rehearsal will be after school, and then there is a group meeting to go over a lab assignment. That evening, you are informed, a group of kids *must* go to the mall to buy something for someone for some urgent reason, although it was all said so fast that you cannot keep track of it. You are not sure who is driving—maybe it's you, or maybe it's your child or one of his friends. You mention an English paper that you thought was due tomorrow, and the reply is, "Oh yeah, don't worry, I'll get it done." As you begin to sink into despair, your child says, "And I need some money, okay?"

5. It is a dangerous neighborhood. There are gunshots late at night, and too many people are hanging around with nothing to do. You are trying your best to make ends meet, but it is not easy. Your child wants to go and hang out; you want to make sure all the schoolwork gets done, and then you need help with your younger children. "But, Ma, all the other kids are going out. They don't have to do their work, or stay home and help out. It's not fair!" Feeling pangs of guilt, your empathy is in a tug-of-war with your goals for your child.

Why were parents put on this earth? To teach, advise, and guide their children? Well, children do not seem to want this guidance too much, and some rebel actively against it. Maybe it's to drive, schedule, feed, and clothe them, buy them things of all kinds, and occasionally remind them about their responsibilities. This seems like what parents spend a lot of time doing, but it does not seem as if this is why we were put on earth. Well, then, why? *To worry!* When we worry a lot, especially when we have not sorted out our own complicated feelings about everything going on in our lives and the lives of our kids, we are likely to use "Worry Words." Unfortunately, such Worry Words, though intended to make things better, often lead to added confusion and emotional upset. Here are some examples of Worry Words:

1. "How many times have I told you to get yourself dressed before you start playing and looking out the window? Do you know how much time you are wasting?"

2. "Don't you remember that I asked you to put the notices for everything on the refrigerator and to write down other things on your schedule? How may times do I have to tell you things before you will listen?"

3. "You will never amount to anything if you lie to me and you do not keep your room from becoming a barnyard. How will you survive in college, when you're away from home?"

4. "This is just what got your brother into trouble—too much socializing, always talking on the phone, not spending enough time with the books."

5. "When I was your age, I was able to do my homework, hold down a job, and still help with the chores around the house. I never hung out with my friends."

We happen to be big fans of parental worrying, and we are worriers ourselves. As all-consuming as parental worrying can be, however, something more is needed. Imagine if, instead of making sure our children learned basic academic skills and sound health habits, we simply *worried* about those things. There would be a lot of uneducated, smelly children running around! We are not so cruel and heartless as to ask parents to give up their worrying; that would be like asking a child to give up a security blanket. Nevertheless, preparing our children for the future requires that we help them develop a strong, positive self-concept, with a feeling of confidence in themselves and (too often missing) the self-discipline and social and emotional intelligence skills and sense of responsibility to back it up.

Accomplishing this requires a household where thoughtfulness and respect for others' feelings are valued and where those values are practiced. The kinds of things that we say, when we are not using our emotional intelligence skills too well, lead children to wonder if we really respect them and value their feelings. Here is a little glimpse at the kinds of things that may be going on in their minds in response to each of the parental scenarios just given:

1. "Time is relative, as Einstein and others have confirmed. Thus, to say that I am 'wasting' time is to imply that time is a fixed entity, a tangible item with specific parameters of use. I feel there is no scientific—or even cross-cultural—basis for your position, and I therefore choose to dress slowly, if at all. I dress, therefore I am."

2. "Based on past experience, I would estimate that you need to say things to me an average of 4.5 times before I have a 50-percent chance of remembering them; the range seems to be between two repetitions and as many as seven or eight. The number decreases if you use written reminders, and, at my age, I also respond well to tangible incentives, like a snack or a book or baseball cards or something like that. Be creative! We are not all blessed with great verbal memories, you know."

3. "If I never will amount to anything, then it certainly doesn't make any sense at all to worry about my work or my room. Thanks! I was feeling badly about not getting to the things I promised I would do, and I was still trying to figure out how to deal with all this stuff at once. No more!"

4. "My brother? What does he have to do with anything we are talking about? I am me, not anyone else. I figure you are you, too. So how about dealing with who we are? Otherwise I will start telling you about my friends' parents and what they do and do not do, which will drive you up the wall."

5. "Well, aren't you just the perfect human being? Never hung out, always working, probably prayed five times a day also, and cleaned all the windows in the projects in your spare time. Since I can't be that good, I may as well just forget trying, and be like other kids."

These are the kinds of things that may cross the minds of children who often hear the well-meaning expressions of parental worry and concern we have given. Our examples are (we hope!) humorous and perhaps a bit exaggerated, to make the point that statements that create "open borders" and a chance for a real flow of words and ideas are more useful than statements that create negative feelings and defensiveness between people in the household.

We know that parents say things in anger and frustration that they would ideally like to "take back." We do this ourselves, as all parents do. What we have found, though, is that there is a balance that represents Emotionally Intelligent Parenting at its best, and this book is about helping you to find and keep that balance in your household.

FAMILY GOALS AND THE TWENTY-FOUR-KARAT PRINCIPLES OF EMOTIONALLY INTELLIGENT PARENTING

So, parents are not perfect. That's no news headline. How do we do the best we can, given all that is going on in our lives and those of our kids? As we said when we presented the Twenty-four-Karat Golden Rule, this is where Emotionally Intelligent

Parenting can help. Contained in that rule are five main principles of Emotionally Intelligent Parenting, which serve as goals for parents and children. Working toward those goals leads to a harmonious family, and attaining them enables children to become self-disciplined and responsible adults. One "secret" to Emotionally Intelligent Parenting is that what is good for parents is also good for children. Progress made by parents results in progress made by their children. We'll begin by introducing the five principles of Emotionally Intelligent Parenting. Each of the chapters in this book will focus on some combination of these principles.

1. Be aware of one's own feelings and those of others.

Feelings are difficult things to be aware of. What is a feeling exactly? Poets, philosophers, and scientists have tried to define it, even though we all know what it is. How do we know what we are feeling? People ask, all the time, "How are you?" and you say, "Fine, how are you?" and they say, "Fine," when this is probably not true for either of you. When was the last time someone asked you how you were and you answered them truthfully? "How are you?" "Well, I'm kind of down. I feel overwhelmed by work, and my wife and I haven't been communicating lately, which leaves me feeling even more lonely, isolated, and unfulfilled." (If you answered this way too often, people would probably stop asking.) The next time someone casually asks you how you are, take a minute to think and give a real answer. Your response may be ignored because the person did not really want to know, but sometimes this can lead to a meaningful interpersonal exchange.

"How are you?" is an important question, whether we ask it to ourselves or others ask it of us. "How are you?" asks us to be able to put our feelings into words, to put labels on them that reflect their variety. Too many children who have problems with behavior also have problems with accurately labeling their feelings. They confuse annoyed and mad, upset and sad, proud and glad, and many others. Once we are able to recognize our different feelings, we have a much better chance of controlling them. Why is this important? At the very least, how you are strongly influences what you do. When you are sad, you are likely to withdraw. When you are happy, you are likely to spread good cheer. But if you don't know—then you're not sure what you are likely to do, and therefore, you're not sure how to manage it.

Similarly, awareness of others' feelings is crucial. If you ask an adolescent how someone else feels, he or she sometimes answers, "I don't know, and why should I care?" They should care, because if they know how someone else feels, they have a better chance of having a positive interaction with them, including, at times, getting what they want. In an adult example, what if you wanted a raise from your boss? It might be helpful to be able to read her mood and know when to ask or when to avoid her. The adolescent who is able to read a teacher's feelings is more likely to get a break on a late assignment, some extra help, and maybe even a better grade than a student who is just as smart in "IQ" but not as smart in "EQ"—emotional intelligence.

2. Show empathy and understand others' points of view.
Empathy is the capacity to share in another's feelings. To do this, one must first be aware of both one's own feelings and the other person's feelings, as noted in Principle Number 1. It is an interesting fact that the better you are at knowing your own feelings, the better you can know another's.

Knowing another's feelings is an important part of developing sensitivity toward others. This is what it means to be "considerate" of others, an idea that is far from new. Many sages have given this advice over the centuries, perhaps most prominently Hillel, who is widely regarded as one of the guiding figures in Judeo-Christian ethical principles, and whose teachings are quoted extensively in the *Ethics of the Fathers:* "Do not judge others until you stand in their shoes." Only by doing this can you understand their point of view *and* their feelings about what is happening. This combination is essential and helps define us as full human beings. For example, when siblings fight, at that moment they may or may not have a sense of each other's perspective, but almost certainly they are not aware of each other's feelings. If they are made aware that their brother or sister also feels sad and hurt, this may temper their anger. Few children wish to make their siblings feel sad. If they can empathize with the other's feelings, they will likely not try to hurt them.

Knowing others' feelings and empathizing with them requires one to be able to read those feelings. This involves both careful listening and reading nonverbal cues. Often, body language and tone of voice convey our emotions more effectively than words. We view empathy as nonverbal emotional understanding of others. The ability to empathize is crucial for parents in dealing with children, and it is vital for children to learn empathy as a positive social skill (not to mention that the capacity for empathy generally makes a person better adjusted emotionally and more successful, especially in romantic relationships).

Understanding others' points of view gives us access to what they might be thinking, how they look at and define a situation, and what they might plan to do. Such understanding, of course, becomes more developed over time. It depends on one's level of cognitive growth, and it also is helped by having a broad range of life experiences. Television and videos can give children a false sense of others' perspectives because they seem like life experiences. But they really are contrived, conjured up by directors, writers, actors, and so on. Our hunch is that kids today act more mature than they truly are because they are exposed to so many "life experiences" in a shallow way, through television and videos.

Young children (and immature adults) tend to view the world in terms of their own wants and needs. As kids get older, around seven or eight years of age, they become better able to negotiate, compromise, and be tolerant. But this process has its ups and downs throughout adolescence, as parents know. Regardless, parents can do a lot every day to teach children how to take different perspectives. With the media, the Internet, and peer culture offering so many confusing and competing messages, we think it is more important than ever for parents to play a strong role in guiding their children's perspective-taking. Much of this requires more than just modeling by parents; it requires explaining their behavior and feelings so that children can better understand "where they are coming from" and not assume they are coming from the same place as television and movie characters. And another reason this is important is that people who are able to see things from different perspectives are usually better able to control impulsive decision-making and are more creative and effective problem-solvers—other important skills we want children to develop.

3. *Regulate and cope positively with emotional and behavioral impulses.*
Daniel Goleman popularized the now-famous Marshmallow Test in his book *Emotional Intelligence*. Walter Mischel is a psychologist who, in the 1960s at Stanford University, posed to four-year-olds the challenge of whether to have a marshmallow now or wait a few minutes until a researcher returned to the room, at which point they would have two marshmallows. Being able to wait—and kids did the cutest things to try to keep from eating the marshmallow—was related to a number of better psychological and behavioral outcomes. Following up these children as they graduated from high school, Mischel found that the students who were able to wait not only had better status on a variety of measures of positive behavior and mental health, but also SAT scores that were on average two hundred points higher than their marshmallow-grabbing age-mates, showing benefits in the academic skills tests so important for college entry.

What's going on here? Are we aiming to increase children's consumption of marshmallow-based products? Or should we help them to develop better self-control and resistance to impulses and temptations of the moment? We suspect the latter, though sometimes hot chocolate with marshmallows sounds a lot better than impulse control. Actually, the Marshmallow Test focuses on a component of coping with behavioral impulses known as delayed gratification, the ability to wait for something. Alas, it is a concept difficult for many adults to master in the age of credit cards, so it is no surprise that it does not come easily to our children. Without the ability to delay gratification, we usually end up with less than we could have had. If you work hard for something, you tend to achieve more and also have the satisfaction of having worked for it. Children who are insecure have an especially difficult time with waiting because they are not sure that the satisfaction will ever come.

Another aspect of self-control is the ability to moderate one's emotional reaction to a situation, whether that reaction is positive or negative. For example, do kids get angry and lose control quickly? Do they become excited and overstimulated, and difficult to calm down? There certainly are times when it feels good to "let it all out," but there are lots of times when this is not the wisest thing to do. After children have inappropriately expressed their feelings—such as by being loud and challenging to a parent—this can trigger reactions that are not usually positive. This, at times, gets parents (or teachers) and children involved in what we call the "yelling spiral." When a child is out of control, the parent usually wants her to stop, which sometimes leads to a loud remark by parents. For some children, this raises their anxiety and activity level instead of lowering it, so they get even more out of control. When this is followed by louder and louder parental reactions, we get into a serious "yelling spiral." Teaching and practicing self-control can be difficult, but working on this can help solve a lot of family problems.

Coping with behavioral impulses is important for obvious reasons. Our instinctive behavioral responses to conflict are often ineffective in coping with such problems. As human beings, we are wired to react to problematic situations with a fight-or-flight response. In prehistoric times, this was of course helpful to our survival. However, in modern society, neither fighting nor running away usually serves us well. We have to use what we know about our own and others' feelings and perspectives to help us better control our impulses. And then we have to start thinking farther ahead.

4. Be positive goal- and plan-oriented.

One of the most important things about human beings is that we can set goals and make plans to reach those goals. This means that, generally, the things parents and children do are goal-oriented. The theory of emotional intelligence tells us this has important implications.

First we must recognize the great power of optimism and hope. When we are in a positive state or a hopeful mood, we are in this state in mind, feelings, and body. There is a distinct bio-chemistry to hopefulness and good spirits, including improved blood flow, cardiovascular and aerobic efficiency, immune system activity, and stress-level reduction. There would be little point in our being oriented toward setting goals if we were not similarly oriented to achieving those goals and deriving benefits from them.

Second, we know that in working toward our goals, we have times when we are more and less effective. Are you an early-morning person? A late-night person? Do you have other "best" times for you to get things done? Part of emotionally intelligent parenting is to recognize these times in ourselves—and in our children—and to work with, not against, such rhythms as much as possible.

Finally, as parents and as people, it would be good if we improved our own goal setting and planning—much as we certainly expect this from our children. We can best accomplish this through self-monitoring and feedback, through keeping track of what we have tried, how well it has worked, and what we can do to improve, across a variety of situations. In our hectic lives, there is a real danger that we will miss feedback opportunities and the lessons they provide. Parents (and kids) are so busy so much of the time that self-reflection seems unproductive and not worth our time. This is a large mistake, based on what we know about Emotionally Intelligent Parenting, and throughout this book, we will present ways to improve parenting through feedback.

Of course, we are not always fully aware of our goals, and they are not always positive. A child may have a goal of revenge for a real or perceived slight. Pursuing revenge, unfortunately, usually will bring about more or new troubles. Parents sometimes have a goal of getting a few moments of peace, when their kids have a goal of getting attention. Need we mention the kinds of difficulties this can lead to?

We must help children understand the meaning of the word *goal*. Some kids relate to the idea of a target; others are helped by the image of a rudder or steering wheel or compass; and still others prefer sports analogies. However it is visualized, being aware of one's goal will help in developing an appropriate plan, and plans are what help us get to our goals. If, for example an adolescent has lied about where he was going, saying he was sleeping over at a friend's house while instead he went to a rock concert, the parent's initial reaction may be to reprimand the adolescent and ground him indefinitely. If, however, the parent formulates a goal before reacting, perhaps to teach the child to be truthful and communicate openly, then a different course of action may be more effective. After all, grounding for an extended period is impractical and often only encourages the child to be sneakier next time!

In this example, it would have also worked better for the child to both formulate a goal (to go to the concert) and develop an effective plan. Teenagers who set up the arrangements to go to a concert without parental permission have engaged in some planning, but usually have not thought it through carefully enough. (As we noted earlier, skills in planning relate to other emotional intelligence areas, such as regulating impulses and delaying gratification.) Later in this book, we will show how the ability to consider obstacles to a plan is crucial for ensuring its success. This applies equally to parents and children.

5. Use positive social skills in handling relationships.

In addition to possessing awareness of feelings, self-control, goal orientation, and empathy, it is important to know how to deal effectively with others. This entails social skills such as communication and problem-solving. In order to communicate, one must not only be able to express oneself in a clear manner, but must also know how to listen and how to give constructive feedback. Again, these are important skills for both parent and child to master.

Another set of skills involves being part of a group. Parents want their family to function well as a group. They also want their kids to have skills for contributing to groups at school, on the job, and in community life. Learning to listen to others carefully and accurately, to take turns, to harmonize different feelings, to compromise, to create consensus, and to state one's ideas clearly are among many social skills that help us work better in groups. And, of course, when members of groups use these skills, those groups work better—including families.

Family vacations are a good time to put such skills to use. A family vacation should be fun for all members of the family, and therefore all should have a say in planning it. Prior to the next vacation, it would be a good idea to have your family sit together and discuss your ideas. Everyone should have a turn to talk while the others listen. From this can come a consensus about where to go and what to do. Of course, compromises may have to be made if Dad wants to go fishing, Mom likes shopping for antiques, Lois yearns to see the ballet, and Artie is into camping. But with good communication skills and a little creative problem-solving, perhaps everyone's needs can be met to some degree. (We will discuss this in greater detail in chapter 6.)

Other important social skills include the ability to solve interpersonal problems and make sound, thoughtful, responsible choices in everyday life, as well as the ability to "bounce back" constructively when we hit inevitable roadblocks and obstacles in our dealings with others.

Think about times when your family has to decide what to do on the weekend. If you are an active family, you may have had to debate between bike trips, rock climbing, skiing and snowboarding, and maybe even a trip to an indoor techno-sports-amusement park for a game of laser tag, a joust with bumper cars, and virtual-reality basketball. This is a time when it helps to have everyone express his or her point of view, try to compromise or take turns, and remember that there is a shared goal—to have fun on the weekend. But of equal importance is how children learn to react when the majority decision goes the wrong way—such as going to a museum instead of a minor-league baseball game. Parents need to recognize that their children will be upset at first, and that it will be hard to reason with them at the moment of greatest disappointment. After they have calmed down, you will be able to help them look ahead to something that they will enjoy for an upcoming weekend. And as your efforts at this are repeated over the course of weeks and months, your children will be better able to look ahead when they don't get their way, equipped with the skills to manage their disappointment and keep focused on their goals, as well as considering the feelings and needs of the rest of the family.

AN INFORMAL MEASURE OF FAMILY MEMBERS' EMOTIONAL INTELLIGENCE

Now you have a sense of what Emotionally Intelligent Parenting involves. To help you get ready for the ideas and activities in this book, take a moment to assess your emotional intelligence and that of your children. Ask yourself the following questions:

My emotional intelligence

1. How well do I know my own feelings? How well do I know the feelings of my family? Think of a recent problem in the family. How were you feeling, or your children, or others involved in the problem?

2. How much empathy do I have for others? Do I express it to them? When was the last time I did this? Am I sure they are aware of what I am doing? Am I able to understand another's point of view even during an argument?

3. How do I cope with anger, anxiety, and other stresses? Am I able to maintain self-control when stressed? How do I behave after a hard day? How often do I yell at others? When are my best and worst times, and do these vary on different days?

4. What goals do I have for myself and my family? What plans do I have for achieving them?

5. How do I deal with problematic, everyday, interpersonal situations? Do I really listen to others? Do I reflect back to people what they are saying? Do I approach social conflicts in a thoughtful manner? Do I consider alternatives before deciding on a course of action?

My child's emotional intelligence

1. How well can my child verbalize feelings? If I ask her how she feels, can she respond with a feeling word, or does she tell me what happened? Can my child identify a range of feelings with gradations in between? Can my child identify feelings in others?

2. How does my child show empathy? When was the last time he seemed to relate to another's feelings? Does he show interest in others' feelings? When I tell him stories about others' misfortunes, how does he react? Can he understand different points of view? Can he see both sides of an argument? Can he do this when in the midst of a conflict?

3. Can my child wait to get what she wants, especially when it is something she *really* wants? Can my child wait to get something that is right there in front of her, but that she can't have now? How well can she tolerate frustration? How does she express anger and other negative feelings?

4. What goals does my child have? What goals would I like her to have? Does my child ever plan things out before doing

something? Have I ever helped her develop a plan for achieving a goal?

5. How does my child resolve conflicts? How independent is he in resolving conflicts? Does he listen, or turn others off? Can he think of different ways of resolving conflicts?

For both yourself and your children, think about areas of strength, the areas you and they are really good at. Give yourself a pat on the back for having these—we mean it!—and praise your children for theirs, as soon as you can. Also think about areas of potential change you would like to focus on. Think of what times of day you are most likely to show these skills, and when you are less likely to show them. These patterns are very important, because we help ourselves when we try to swim with the current, as opposed to going against it.

You may find you are not sure of some of the answers to the questions we pose. This is more common than not, because we are asking parents to think about things a little differently from the ways they are used to thinking about them. One way to get some answers is to videotape a (non-offensive) sitcom and then watch it with your child. Or read a story to your child. At various points in the tape or story, pause and discuss the following:

- How the main character is feeling.
- How the other characters are feeling and what they are thinking.
- How your child feels about the characters' feelings.
- What the different characters' goals are, and what your child thinks the characters' plans might be.
- How your child thinks the characters handled a situation.
- What your child thinks was good about how the characters handled the situation, and what the characters could have done better.

Don't be surprised if, the first few times, your child has difficulty responding, or even has a negative response. That is why you are reading this book. We will help provide you with opportunities and experiences in the course of everyday parenting to help your children develop the skills to answer these questions not only for stories, but also for real life. What this requires on your part is Emotionally Intelligent Parenting.

What Emotionally Intelligent Parenting Is...and What It Is Not

Emotionally Intelligent Parenting is not parenting-by-the-numbers. Detailed, step-by-step approaches—"Five Weeks to a New Household," "Seven Steps to Angelic Children," "How to Become the Model Parent"—may look good on paper and sound inviting when authors and experts talk about them. But these types of approaches rarely seem to work in *your* house. We want to emphasize that this is not your failing.

Like all of the most rewarding and meaningful things we do in life, parenting has many layers and levels of challenge and richness. Emotionally Intelligent Parenting recognizes that it is the sum total of what we do—in matters both large and small, day after day—that can create a healthier balance in households and in relationships with children. We must act in ways that emphasize the importance of feelings and help us and our children handle a range of emotions with a degree of self-control, as opposed to acting impulsively or allowing ourselves to get too carried away with our feelings (what Daniel Goleman refers to as "emotional hijacking").

For some children, life is harsh and unsafe; for others, it is tension-packed. In either case, a loss of control on their part can mean loss of privileges, loss of after-school or mentoring activities, loss of job opportunities, or even placement in special school settings or living arrangements. Children need the skills to grow up in a positive, nurturing, opportunity-rich environment.

Emotionally Intelligent Parenting helps make that more likely.

It is not about micro-managing your children, or yourselves as parents. Nor is it about having broad principles or "philosophies" of parenting, with no clues about how to implement them.

The remainder of this book is organized so that each chapter begins with a brief outline of the Emotional Intelligence principles that will be emphasized in that chapter. Because emotions, thoughts, and actions intertwine, our strategies for building Emotionally Intelligent Parenting must use several principles together. This is neither simplistic nor overly complex, but realistic and practical. It also allows parents to choose among various suggestions. It's better to use a few principles consistently, than be overwhelmed by trying to use them all at once.

GET READY FOR A JOURNEY: THE PLAN OF THE BOOK

You are about to embark on a journey, to look at different aspects of your family life. You don't really have to read this book from start to finish; there may be certain chapters that you want to start out with because they seem to address issues of greatest concern to you. Here is the layout:

In chapter 2, we'll look at how your family is set up. What can you do to make it more likely that family time is a time for caring, sharing, and problem-solving together? How can it be a less stressful time for everyone? We'll introduce ways to bring more fun and laughter into your family life. In chapter 3, we'll show you how you can talk to your kids so that they actually will be more thoughtful and respond to you more actively and reasonably. Its guiding principles will be of great use to you, no matter how old your children are. They should create noticeable improvements in your household. Chapter 4 will look at discipline, but from the point of view of Emotionally Intelligent Parenting. How can we create a sense of self-control and responsibility in our kids that they take with them, and not just use when they are being "watched"?

Chapter 5 goes a step further and shares some of the most effective ways of building children's self-control and social skills and helping them to be less impulsive and more thoughtful. In that chapter we present "FIG TESPN"—a problem-solving strategy you won't forget! In chapter 6 we consider situations that are a bit more complicated and require thoughtful problem-solving on the part of both parents and children. Here the focus will be on the key difference between having good ideas and actually putting them into responsible action. Parents will enjoy some of the ways we help everyone get more creative about dealing with situations and solving problems. Chapter 7 gives us a chance to present examples of how the skills of Emotionally Intelligent Parenting can be used by parents and children to deal with challenging everyday parenting situations, especially those that center around school, from kickball to choices about careers and college and everything in between—including homework, of course.

Tough issues are tackled in chapter 8, where we focus on how to adapt the principles of Emotionally Intelligent Parenting to reach hard-to-reach children. We select what we have found to be the most powerful family times to "reach" children, and we show how to put all the principles to work naturally. The point we make is that in an age of violence, AIDS, and drugs, we all have to make extra efforts to reach all kids, and we share the best strategies we know.

In chapter 9 is a series of "Sound EQ Parenting Bites"—examples of brief Emotionally Intelligent Parenting answers to common questions parents ask us. They cover such topics as parental anger, car rides, homework, bedtimes, disagreements between parents, what to do when your kids are very sad, how to get everyone out of the house in the morning, how to set limits with teenagers, and how to handle lying, cheating, and other dishonesty.

You are now ready to embark! Read and enjoy. Share these ideas and examples with relatives and friends. Above all, try out new things and make them work for you. We've seen the principles of Emotionally Intelligent Parenting make a difference in many homes, and we know they can make a difference in yours.

Chapter 2

Creating a Sharing, Caring, Problem-Solving Family

■ ■ ■

Sharing perspectives, discussing feelings, linking feelings to events in the family—this is what allows families to be supportive resources for children. When parents set a positive tone, and when they help children solve problems, rather than provide answers or make all the decisions, children are much more likely to develop a sense of responsibility.

Making this happen in families follows from some relatively small things, done consistently and often over a period of years. In particular, this chapter addresses how to take strong and not-so-strong family feelings and keep them from getting out of hand or being misunderstood or, just as harmful, suppressed or ignored. In the language of Emotional Intelligence, parents themselves must avoid being "emotionally hijacked"—that is, allowing themselves to be so overwhelmed by strong feelings that they act without careful thinking—and be clear about the values and rules that are most important to the family. One of these must emphasize caring about one another's doings, experiences, ideas, and the feelings that accompany them. It is too easy, in this age of information overload, to get distracted and focus on trivia. One of the most critical jobs of parenting is to help children grow up to be socially skilled and emotionally healthy. Family rules, times for family discussion and problem-solving, and a spirit of goodwill and cooperation set children on a constructive and positive path.

Emotional Intelligence Principles Highlighted in This Chapter's Activities

☞ 1. Be Aware of One's Own Feelings and Those of Others
☞ 2. Show Empathy and Understand Others' Points of View
   3. Regulate and Cope Positively with Emotional and Behavioral Impulses
   4. Be Positive Goal- and Plan-Oriented
☞ 5. Use Positive Social Skills in Handling Relationships

WHO ARE WE AS A FAMILY? WHAT DOES IT MEAN TO BE A MEMBER OF OUR FAMILY?

With everything that families are facing, steps must be taken to keep kids from feeling adrift and confused by their lives. Families should do more than provide places to do homework, arrange car pools for soccer games, or serve as stopovers for an occasional meal. We have found it enormously helpful to encourage families to set up a Family Motto, a Family Mission Statement, and a Family Constitution (or, as we will discuss, Rules of the Road).

A caring family is grounded in positive relationships, and a critical basis for those relationships is parents' values and goals. What does it mean to be a member of this family? What beliefs or Big Ideas do we have in common? Naturally, these will change as one's family matures, but let's take as an example one dad, with four children ranging in age from two to eleven years. He proudly says that you can go over to any one of his kids and ask them, "What do we do in our family?" and they will answer, "We share." This is just one example of a Family Motto, a short phrase that everyone understands and can use as a guide to everyday behavior and choices. Some others we have encountered include "We don't hurt other people," "We care about other people," "We listen to each other," "We have respect for others and for other points of view."

A Family Mission Statement is a bit more involved. When one's kids are young, it is often mainly for the benefit of the parents, to keep them focused on what is most important during the busy time of establishing homes, careers, and new families. Here is an example of a Family Mission Statement:

"We are a family dedicated to learning, laughing, growing together, sharing among ourselves, and sharing with others."

This provides some real guidelines for busy families. Some may prefer to add other words, like "caring," and families with strong religious beliefs may want to reflect those in their statements.

A Family Constitution usually contains some more specific principles for handling everyday issues. Here are some examples:

"We will use our words and not fight."

"We will do our homework before we watch TV or get on the Internet."

"The TV will not be on when we eat, except on special occasions we all agree upon."

"On Sundays, we all attend church."

"When friends come into the house, they will take off their shoes."

"No food in the bedrooms!"

"When someone hurts your feelings, don't hold it in—tell them about it as nicely as you can."

"At mealtimes, everybody helps."

"At dinner, we give thanks for our food."

"Grandparents and teachers are always to be treated with the greatest respect!"

"No one may put down another member of the family, especially in front of other people."

If you think of the United States Constitution as a model, you know that it does not go into great detail, but it does provide an indication of rights and responsibilities and core values. We recommend that you start off with a Family Motto and then add a Constitution of maybe three to four points. Post it prominently, refer to it, and then, after you have lived with it for a while, you can "amend" it as desired. Brainstorm with your family about what the points might be, and then figure out as a group how to get them down to three or four. Doing this will create some investment on the part of your kids, and it works much better than when parents create an edict from on high.

How do we set the stage for discussing these ways of defining a family? One way to begin is to establish the idea of Sharing Time. The idea is simple: it is a time for family members to take turns sharing how they are feeling, and to talk about important events of the day or upcoming events (or past events) that are on people's minds. Often this is best accomplished at the dinner table or in a car. It begins by creating rules for listening to others and for having everyone's point of view heard. Drawing from the Guiding Principles presented earlier, we know that Sharing Time will work when people feel it is safe to share. They do not want to be insulted, punished, or laughed at for their ideas. Without a sense of safety and a history of sharing ideas and feelings, it is hard to get participation in creating a genuine Family Motto or Mission Statement.

Another way of sharing is through a Family Journal. This is a looseleaf book left out on the table for people to write down their thoughts, experiences, questions, worries—whatever they would like to share. Others can write back to them. Drawings certainly have a place in such a journal, as might pictures cut out from newspapers or magazines. A more structured version is a Family Diary. Here, family members are asked each day to record meaningful or interesting events that have brought about strong feelings, positive or negative. Parents also can leave messages for kids, reminding them about homework and chores and appointments/meetings, and kids can remind parents of when and where they have to drive that day, who else is being picked up, and which homework has to be checked first, as well as reasons for why certain chores will not be done. Some families use dry-erase marker boards for this, and erase the entries to start fresh each day. However, some will appreciate the permanence of a chronicle.

Finally, some families focus on a Family Calendar. This is an existing or computer-created calendar with large boxes so that upcoming events can be written in, and past events can be recorded. It's a good way of keeping track of birthdays and other remembrances. Many families find that looking back at their calendars over the years (these are well worth saving!) yields a treasure trove of memories and family history.

MY KIDS WON'T BUY THIS— SO WHAT DO I DO?

For a lot of reasons, some children don't make it easy on parents who try to carry out something like this for the first time. One of us had this kind of experience when introducing a family sharing time. There was silence, ridicule, lack of cooperation, angry conversation—it was neither easy nor fun. Persisting was not easy. It was hard not to be defensive or angry in return, or to forget the whole thing. Persistence is vital; if the parent does not believe in its value, it cannot succeed in the long run.

There are several ways to deal with kids' scoffing. First, choose your timing carefully. Don't spring it suddenly on your family, and don't interfere with an already-promised event or outing. Start at a time when your family is likely to be together already. Some parents have found that a good time to start talking about a Family Motto or Mission Statement or family sharing is when everyone is in a restaurant. The public setting helps tone down negativity and prevents escaping to one's room. Another approach is to use E-mail. With teenagers especially, surprisingly good and rational conversations take place in that medium, often better than talking face to face. Let your kid comment on the idea, and work gradually toward putting it into practice.

With teenagers and some hard-to-reach children, bartering can be effective. Make a deal that you will try not to do one of the things that bothers your child most if he or she will engage in a discussion with you about this, and give your ideas a try. Sandra and Harry Choron, in their *Book of Lists for Kids* (Houghton Mifflin, 1995), provide some ideas of the top things parents do that kids find rude. Here are some examples from their lists, and some from ours, that you can offer to refrain from doing if your kids will agree to try some family sharing, journals, diaries, or calendars:

- Criticize your child in front of his or her friends.
- Tell your child's private secrets to other family members.
- Open your child's mail.
- Ask your child to perform for company.
- Hang around when your child's friends come over, get too "chummy."
- Forget your child's friends' names, or confuse one friend with another.
- Invade your child's privacy by coming into his or her room without knocking.
- Ask your child's friends lots of personal questions (i.e., about their parents, jobs, or possessions).
- Ignore your child when your own friends visit.
- Ask about the same things related to school more than once in the same hour.
- Make critical comments about what your child listens to on the radio.
- Nag your child about getting more sleep while also telling him or her to do more schoolwork.
- Complain about your child's eating patterns.

An effective way of engaging adolescents in a Family Journal is to capitalize on their curiosity. Let them know that they can read the journal whether or not they contribute. Use the journal as a place to reflect on or praise your child. Gradually, put into the journal a question that you have for him or her. We have found that curiosity is often more powerful than resistance. Don't be surprised to find answers to your questions in the journal—and don't say, "I knew you would write in the journal eventually." If you do, they are likely to stop writing.

Regardless of how you go about it, you will find that a sense of humor helps. There are few things more valuable to Emotionally Intelligent Parenting than the ability to see the lighter side of things. We will share some ideas about how to do this later in the chapter. (Please note that children who are alienated from family activities and even somewhat anti-parent will require a bit more specialized work—we will address this issue in chapter 8.)

Once we begin to develop a sense of sharing, caring, and family problem-solving, it is time to take out the Road Map.

A ROAD MAP TO BECOMING A CARING, SHARING, PROBLEM-SOLVING FAMILY

The idea of the Road Map comes from Eliot Malomet, a teacher, rabbi, and parent. As parents travel down the Emotionally Intelligent Parenting highway, there are going to be a number of signs along the way. Attending to those signs is one of the best things parents can do if they want to reach their destination. Here are some of the most important signs you will see, along with some Emotionally Intelligent Parenting travel tips.

STOP!

How do we show kids we care? Paradoxically, it is not by giving them everything they want, or by constantly going out of our way to do things for them. In truth, when parents do not provide limits for children, children think they don't care about them. While they will never come out and say this, children need adults to set some boundaries and guidelines. They need adults to be adults, which means to take responsibility for the well-being of our children and to make some decisions and choices based on our wisdom, experiences, and values. Every parent needs to have some points that are not negotiable, especially as their kids enter the teenage years and face decisions with very serious consequences.

REDUCE SPEED—SHARP CURVES!

School has started. There is homework in three subjects. There are tryouts for sports teams. There is a quiz in math, of all things. It's Grandpa Lou's birthday, and Bubbe and Zeide's anniversary party. And are those ants you see crawling around in the light fixture? When things are overwhelming, it's necessary to slow down. Trying to do it all, all the time, is a recipe for stress and turmoil. The only question is which medical or mental health professional you will end up seeing. Emotionally intelligent parents know how to read the signs of their own feelings and those of their children. They know that when there are sharp curves ahead, it is necessary to reduce speed, steer very carefully, and keep one's eyes on the road ahead and both hands on the wheel.

INFORMATION AHEAD

There are many times when parents simply do not know what to do. It is an act of emotional intelligence to put aside stubbornness or false pride and find out what you need to know. You probably have friends whose ideas about parenting, at least in certain areas, you find worthwhile. Maybe one of your relatives knows a technique or two. Other sources include school psychologists, guidance counselors, social workers, and health educators. Pediatricians have lots of experience in dealing with kids, and know referral sources. Such magazines as *Parents*, *Parenting*, and *Child*, as well as sites on the Internet maintained by their publishers and others, often contain useful parenting information.

Just as men, in particular, have a reputation for not wanting to ask for directions when lost, parents often show the same tendency. Get off the road and get some new directions.

INSPECTION STATION

Well, we are taking a slightly different point of view on this from what you might think. An Inspection can be viewed as a time to see what is good and right about something, rather than as a chance only to uncover problems. Too often, in the name of efficiency, parents reflect society's impatience to identify a problem and solve it. A parenting tune-up is oriented around the following questions: When are my kids at their best? When am I at my best as a parent? When are my kids at their worst? When am I at my worst as a parent?

By asking these questions, and by starting with a focus on our "best," we are examining what are known, in Emotional Intelligence theory, as "optimal performance" states. This simply means that we all have times when we are sharpest, clearest, and most focused in the things we are doing. It may be hard to find such a time, and easier to identify times when we are at our worst. Some examples may include the moment you walk in the door after work, times when you are awakened too early on the weekend, when it is very late and you are tired, before you have read the mail and checked for urgent E-mail. Sometimes parents are at their best in late mornings and early evenings.

And of course, the same is true for kids. Is it fair to hit them with an adult agenda at their worst time of day? Can this possibly go well? Not really. By respecting and understanding our own and our kids' "bests" and "worsts," we can build these into the family routine and prevent a lot of emotional turmoil that is neither necessary nor productive. Does this mean we will sometimes have to wait to say what is on our minds? Yes. Does it mean that our kids will sometimes have to wait to ask us for favors? Yes. It also means that there will be better and worse times for family discussions and serious decision-making. These will change as our families grow and life routines become more or less involved or divergent.

We also have some advanced tune-up equipment we can recommend. Think about your children's strengths. Some are not the best talkers. But they express themselves well through music, drawing, or painting, or by acting something out in person or with toys or props, or by building something. (Parents may be familiar with this if their children's schools have had workshops in "the Multiple Intelligences," based on the work of Howard Gardner, a Harvard psychologist and author.) The Inspection Station sign gives parents a chance to do a check on how their kids *are*, not on how they want them to be or would like them to be. With this information, parents are better equipped to handle those sharp curves. Be sure your kids have time to engage in things that speak to and uplift their spirits. It's up to parents to make sure their children's strengths do not get overlooked by demands that tap areas that are not so strong.

This subject is important enough to justify a brief detour for some examples. In one household, the family decided that Mom would wear a button that said "Beware of Parent!" when she walked in the door, as a way of warning her kids not to bombard her with questions and requests until she had ten minutes to take off her shoes and look through the mail. In another household, a cardboard cutout of a stoplight hangs on the wall by the front door. As each child comes in, she or he puts up the red, yellow, or green signal to let Mom and Dad know what kind of day it was, or at least whether she or he is ready to talk about things. The red and green signals are obvious. Yellow means there are things to talk about, but proceed with caution and be prepared to stop.

An example of how to enhance strengths comes from a child who has never been a good math student but loves to draw. A typical parenting strategy might be to make sure he sits down and gets his math done before anything else, especially before he "forgets" or avoids it. Well, we have found it far more effective to make an arrangement whereby ten or fifteen minutes of real math work is followed, if the child so chooses, by a ten-minute drawing or music break. Alternating areas of weakness and frustration with areas of strength seems to have a positive carryover into the trouble spot: discouragement is less intense, frustration less severe, avoidance and fights about homework are cut back significantly, and confidence grows. For some kids, you will find that they need a break from writing assignments to do math puzzles; for others, a word search puzzle after three long division problems or equations is like a chocolate bar—well, maybe not quite.

These strategies are especially important if one or more of your children has a learning problem, an emotional or behavioral difficulty, physical challenges, problems in paying attention, or other areas in which his or her weaknesses are on display often. We have to provide a balance, and we do that by making sure that strengths also get a chance to be on regular display.

TOLL PLAZA AHEAD

In every family, tasks and chores must be done so that the household can continue. These include earning money, cleaning, putting things away, doing laundry, shopping, cooking, washing dishes, repairing, getting medical and dental checkups, recycling and garbage disposal, planting, watering, taking care of pets, and paying bills. This is the "price" of family life. It is like a toll we pay to get from one side of a bridge to another, or to travel a distance on a turnpike. It is the price we have to pay to get from where we are now to where we want to be. But tolls also make a contribution. They allow the pathway to be maintained. They enable things that we are really looking forward to to take place. Seeing these tasks in this way helps family members share in the work without thinking of it as a chore. It makes a contribution to our family. We all make contributions of different kinds, all of which are important; to be a family, we need them all. And if we have to do others' work, it leaves less time for our own, and it makes it harder for the family to get where it wants to go. We pay a toll not as a penalty, but as a necessary part of getting where we want to go.

YIELD

It gets harder and harder to keep track of everything our kids are doing. Even when schools have voice-mail and communication systems where teachers leave messages for parents with children's assignments and upcoming school events, it is still hard for many parents to be sure what their children could, should, or must do. Should they do a five-page report instead of a four-page one? Do they need to check all of the math problems and show their work? Is it really okay if a lab report is written up in a way that is not as neat as parents would like? Could there actually be a teacher who does not mind collecting assignments ripped out of a spiral notebook? Why isn't the second half of chapter six included on the test?

When parents aren't sure, it makes a lot of sense to use the Yield sign. This means you are suggesting that your children proceed, but with caution. You do not have reasons to tell them to come to a full stop. The situation doesn't require it. So, you yield to what they are saying. This certainly builds up a feeling of trust. It also gives you one less thing to keep close track of. With school, for example, over time and in conversations you will have with the teaching staff, you can determine whether you are hearing about all the things going on in school that should be coming to your attention. In this high-speed world, parents must "yield" more often—but never take your hands off the wheel, your foot off the pedal, or your eyes off the road.

FOUR-WAY STOP

Every family needs down time. This need is reflected in many religious and spiritual traditions. Fridays, Saturdays, and Sundays are "sacred" days for different religions. These are occasions to depart from the routine and spend time as a family in common observance of shared beliefs. This notion also embodies emotional intelligence. Family members need to keep a sense of empathy and perspective for one another. We do not want too much time to go by without finding out what everyone else is doing, how they are feeling about what is going on in their lives, or what stress, deadlines, projects, and positive goals are looming just ahead. The Four-Way Stop sign is something that parents need to put up when they feel the family is moving in too many directions at once—either away from or even toward each other. We need to stop at our corners, take time to communicate, reflect, plan, and then proceed with some better sense of order and knowledge of where others in the family are headed. This way, we are less likely to lose sight of our loved ones—or crash. How do parents do this? Establish a time for a Four-Way Stop. Next Wednesday night, we are all eating dinner together. No one is running out for any meetings. If you have a meeting, be prepared to be late. If you have homework, plan in advance to start it later. Many families have a hard time doing this on a regular basis. Strive to find some regular times, and be sure not to let more than a couple of weeks go by without one. (Traveling parents—you can at least call in during these times; speakerphones are now pretty common. If you are a cyberfamily, you can probably be in touch via the Internet.)

SCENIC OVERLOOK

Part of Emotionally Intelligent Parenting is to realize that family members need to take a break from the usual routine once in a while and savor the beauty of the world around them. And isn't that what a scenic overlook is? It's that spot on the road created for a brief stop to appreciate a natural view. For hectic travelers on the parenting superhighway, it is good to take a moment to appreciate things that we too often just rush by without seeing. Take time to look at the night sky. Look carefully at some of the pictures in your home and reappreciate them. Do the same for pictures in your photo albums or photo shoe boxes, or for old family videos. Take a walk around your house and notice what you have not seen before, or lately. Even in a city, there will be plants struggling to come up through sidewalks, trees and flowers that call out to be noticed, pigeons that refuse to fly away because they feel the sidewalk is as much theirs as yours. In the suburbs or in rural areas, you may have more natural beauty around you, but that does not mean you have taken the time to savor it, to look at it with wonder, to allow it to help you and your family come to greater peace with each other as you recognize that all is not as it seems to be, that there are wonders close by if we choose to attend to them, and that we miss a lot when we do not pause from the rush of our lives and gain a broader perspective on where we are and what we are doing.

LAST SERVICE STATION FOR 2,000 MILES

Well, this might be a slight exaggeration. But these kinds of signs prompt us to check our car's fuel tank. The family fuel tank is its values and rules, so we should not go for too long without picking up the hood and checking our Family Motto, Mission Statement, or Constitution. Are they still in working order? Do they need a little grease? Is there a part or two that might use replacing? Could more extensive repairs be needed? Better to find out now than in the middle of nowhere. Preventive maintenance is a good idea for families, as it is for cars. Whether it's the gauges telling you to make a stop, or if the ride just does not quite feel right, or when you know it's time for a routine check, take that time, look things over, and make the changes you think are necessary. Then your family can get back on the road, cruising along more smoothly.

HOW TO LIGHTEN UP HOUSEHOLDS WITH FAMILY HUMOR

How do you feel about laughter? Do you think it's a sign of frivolity, lack of seriousness, maybe even irreverence or disrespect? Well, that may be true at times. But we think that laughter is missing from the lives of too many families, and that it's the single thing that can really make a difference in terms of creating a caring, problem-solving environment.

According to Edward Dunkelblau, president of the American Association for Therapeutic Humor, research shows that kids laugh in excess of two hundred times per day. Adults laugh an average of about fifteen times daily. What happened to those 185 laughs? What a huge loss! Families that laugh together can enjoy one another's company, put ideas forward that might not be perfect or well thought out, make mistakes without being afraid of being ridiculed—and, believe it or not, they are healthier for it. We can light up our lives by lightening up our households.

Take the following test, which we found in *The Free Spirit Newsletter: News and Views on Growing Up* (vol. 4, no. 3, January–February 1991).

Read this paragraph aloud:

Ha ha ha ha ha ha. Hee hee hee. Har-de-har-har. Nyuck nyuck nyuck. Ho ho ho ho. Ha ha hee hee har har nyuck ho ho. Tee hee hee hee ha ha ho ho ho ho ho ha ha ha ha ha. Nyuck nyuck nyuck. Ha ha ha ha har-de-har ho ho ho hee hee hee hee giggle giggle ha ha. Ho ho ho ho ho ha ha ha ha hee hee hee. Ha ha. Ha!

Did you start to laugh? Maybe smile a bit? Maybe you want to fiddle around with this so it works better for you. Here is one adaptation we like:

Ho ho ho ho ho! Har-har-har-de-har-har. Nyuck nyuck nyuck nyuck nyuck. Ha ho he hoo de-har nyuck hoo har ha ho. He nyuck de-har har. Ho de-ho ho ha ha de-hoo-ha. De-nyuck ha-hoo yi-yeh shmoo de-he ha. Halva tee hee hee ha ho ho. Har-nyuck nyuck-har de hoo nyuck ho ha har ho. Hoo hoo!

Any better? Well, you and your family can take turns trying to do even better! Now, why is this even worth trying? Great and healthy things happen to our bodies when we laugh. Our heart rate goes up, our immune system is activated, hormones are pumped out that make us more alert, and oxygen goes to our brains, which seems to help us think a bit sharper and see things more clearly. Our muscles relax, and our digestive system works better. Nyuck nyuck!

Other good things follow from all this. Stress levels go down. The air is less tense. We are freed to be more creative and broaden our point of view; become more capable of empathetic feelings; we become less hostile, and our ability to make sound decisions and resolve conflicts improves. This is not really a miracle; it is what Emotionally Intelligent Parenting is about: recognizing how our kids—and we—are set up biologically, emotionally, intellectually, and working with this knowledge, not against it or in ignorance of it.

So let's take a few moments and see if we can add an HQ—Humor Quotient—to your family's EQ.

Keep track of good jokes (or even lousy ones). Here are three types, adapted from *Free Spirit*:

MOTHER: Keesha, don't be selfish. Let your brother share the bicycle with you.
KEESHA: But, Mother, I do. I ride down the hill, and he rides up.

■ ■ ■

STUDENT: I'm having trouble with this test. I have amnesia.
TEACHER: How long have you had it?
STUDENT: Had what?

LEO: Mother, I got a hundred in two subjects!
MOTHER: Really? What were they?
LEO: A forty in history and a sixty in math.

And how about a knock-knock joke or two? Using names in ways people don't expect can be fun:

Knock knock.
Who's there?
Zeke.
Zeke who?
Zeke and you shall find.

■ ■ ■

Matthew.
Matthew who?
Matthew is pinching my foot.

■ ■ ■

Althea.
Althea who?
Althea later.

■ ■ ■

Noah.
Noah who?
Noah good place to eat?

Another pattern involves listening to a word carefully or, if reading, focusing on the sound more than the appearance:

Tuna.
Tuna who?
Tuna violin and it will sound better.

Denial.
Denial who?
Denial is a river in Egypt.

Young children like jokes that spark their imagination and use familiar things like colors, letters, animals, and body parts in new ways. For example:

What color can you eat?
Orange.

■ ■ ■

What color is sad?
Blue.

■ ■ ■

What flower got up?
Rose.

■ ■ ■

What letter stings?
B.

■ ■ ■

What letter is wet?
C.

■ ■ ■

What letter looks at you?
I.

■ ■ ■

What letter has to go to the bathroom?
P.

What letter can you drink?
T.

. . .

What letter is not me?
U.

. . .

What animal is naked?
Bear.

. . .

What animal has laryngitis?
Horse.

. . .

What part of your body is the smartest?
Nose. (It knows the most.)

. . .

What part of your body hops?
Hair. (Hare, like a rabbit.)

. . .

What part of your body is a flower?
Two lips. (Tulips.)

Jokes that are paradoxical and bring inanimate and animal characters to life capture the imagination of many middle-school students. Here is a cute joke from David Shaffer in Illinois, courtesy of Patty Wooten on the Internet:

A panda sauntered into an Old West saloon and told the bartender, "Give me a sandwich and a beer." The bartender had met a lot of strange characters and knew it was important to keep his cool. Without a word, he slapped a ham sandwich and a cold frosty one in front of the bear. The panda, having been on the trail for some time, gulped down the sandwich and washed it down with the beer. Then he pulled out his six-shooter and plugged the piano player right between the eyes.

The panda holstered his gun and began to leave. The bartender pulled his shotgun out from under the bar and yelled, "What's the big idea?"

The bear slowly turned and said, "Well, what do you expect?"

"I sure didn't expect you to shoot my piano player!" the bartender yelled. "Good help is hard to find, and besides, you still owe me for lunch."

"I'm a panda," replied the bear. "Look it up." And with that, he left.

The bartender was too amazed to do anything. He put his shotgun on the bar, reached down, pulled out his dictionary, and turned to the entry for *panda*. "I'll be!" he muttered, realizing there was nothing he could do. There it was, in black and white, written by an authority no less than Webster himself:

"Panda. A large, bearlike animal of the mountains of China and Tibet, with distinctive white and black markings. Eats shoots and leaves."

Another form of humor takes a new look at something familiar. In this case, Patty Wooten takes a cyber-glance at books. This goes over well with teens of all ages, and especially those who love computers.

Introducing the new Bio-Optic Organized Knowledge device (BOOK)

BOOK is a revolutionary breakthrough in technology: no wires, no electric circuits, no batteries, nothing to be connected or switched on. It's so easy to use, even a child can operate it. Compact and portable, it can be used anywhere—even sitting in an armchair by the fire—yet it is powerful enough to hold as much information as a CD-ROM disc. Here's how it works:

BOOK is constructed of sequentially numbered sheets of finely pressed wood derivatives, known also as paper (recyclable), each capable of holding thousands of bits of information.

The pages are locked together with a custom-fit device called a binder, which keeps the sheets in their correct sequence. Opaque Paper Technology (OPT) allows manufacturers to use both sides of the sheet, doubling the information density and cutting costs. Experts are divided on the prospects for further increases in information density; for now, BOOKs containing more information simply use more pages.

Each sheet is scanned optically, registering information directly into the human brain. Moving along the information stream is carried out digitally—a flick of the finger takes one to the next sheet. BOOK may be taken up at any time and used merely by opening it.

BOOK never crashes or requires rebooting, though, like other display devices, it can become unusable if dropped overboard. The "browse" feature allows you to move instantly to any sheet, and move forward or backward as you wish. Many come with an "index" feature, which pinpoints the exact location of any selected information for instant retrieval.

An optional "BOOKmark" accessory allows you to open BOOK to the exact place you left it in a previous session—even if the BOOK has been closed.

BOOKmarks fit universal design standards; thus, a single BOOKmark can be used in BOOKs by various manufacturers. Conversely, numerous BOOKmarks can be used in a single BOOK if the user wants to store numerous views at once.

The number is limited only by the number of pages in the BOOK. You can also make personal notes next to BOOK text entries with an optional programming tool, the Portable Erasable Nib Cryptic Intercommunication Language Stylus (PENCILS).

Portable, durable, and affordable, BOOK is being hailed as a precursor of a new entertainment wave. Also, BOOK's appeal seems so certain that thousands of content creators have committed to the platform and investors are reportedly flocking. Look for a flood of new titles soon.

Here is another bit of humor that inspires teenagers to create similar clever looks at the world around them:

An Owed to the Spelling Checker

I have a spelling checker
It came with my PC
It plane lee marks four my revue
Miss steaks aye can knot sea.

Eye ran this poem rat threw it,
Your sure Lee reel glad two no.
Its vary polished in it's weigh
My checker tolled me sew.

A checker is a bless sing,
It freeze yew lodes of thyme.
It helps me right awl stiles two reed,
And aides me when aye rime

Butt now bee cause my spelling
Is checked with such grate flare,
Their are know faults with in my cite
Of nun eye am a wear.

Two rite with care is quite a feet
Of witch won should be prod.
And wee mussed dew the best wee can,
Sew flaws are knot aloud.

Sow ewe can sea why aye dew prays
Such soft ware four pea seas.
And why I brake in two averse
Wayne righting wet eye pleas.

From Patty Wooten, Jest for the Health of It
(http://www.mother.com/JestHome)

Humor for older teenagers is, well, hard to characterize. But one thing that always brings a smile—even if accompanied by groans—is a pun, especially a bad one. Here are a few for older teens:

A doctor made it his regular habit to stop off at a bar for a hazelnut daiquiri on his way home. The bartender knew of his habit, and would always have the drink waiting at precisely 5:03 P.M. One afternoon, as the end of the workday approached, the bartender was dismayed to find that he was out of hazelnut extract. Thinking quickly, he threw together a daiquiri made with hickory nuts and set it on the bar. The doctor came in at his regular time, took one sip of the drink, and exclaimed, "This isn't a hazelnut daiquiri!" "No, I'm sorry," replied the bartender, "it's a hickory daiquiri, Doc."

■ ■ ■

An old Indian chief had a stomachache that wouldn't go away. He summoned the tribal shaman. The spiritualist gave him a leather thong two feet long. "Chew on the thong every day for twenty minutes, until you've eaten the whole thing, and you will be cured." The old chief took weeks to finally eat the whole thing, but still had the stomachache. So he summoned the shaman again. "Did you eat the thong?" asked the shaman.

The chief replied, "Yes, the thong is gone, but the malady lingers on."

■ ■ ■

A guy goes to a psychiatrist. "Doc, I keep having these alternating recurring dreams. First I'm a teepee; then I'm a wigwam; then I'm a teepee; then I'm a wigwam. It's driving me crazy. What's wrong with me?"

The doctor replied, "It's very simple. You're two tents."

What is the point of these jokes? First, some may be funny to you. Second, they help lighten up the family atmosphere. They make a statement that humor—even attempted humor—is a valuable part of a household, and a contributor to family health.

Here are some other ways to bring humor into schoolwork and homework:

- Have a bulletin board in the house for school-related cartoons and comics. Maybe you can even get one at school.
- Cut off cartoon captions and write your own. This can be a family or class activity.
- For current events, cut out pictures and supply your own quotes.
- Have a humor corner in your house or classroom. Pictures, books, or whatever else people find funny would go there.
- Have a laugh break. This can really help with homework, especially when kids are stuck. Short tapes or segments of audiotapes or videotapes or time to read from humorous books or cartoons can really make a huge difference. It is hard, frustrating, and ineffective to just sit there and "keep trying" when one is truly stuck. Humor opens up new pathways and perspectives. It is not a waste of valuable time!

Humor is not the same for kids of all ages. Now that we have seen a few examples, it's worth a brief review of how our perceptions of humor change over the years. Through the preschool years, humor is connected to ongoing play and physical activity. "Acting silly" often results in big laughs, for kids and for adults watching them. Kids also love to see adults act silly, do the unexpected, or exaggerate. Ed Dunkelblau encourages parents to use props—funny hats, things worn backwards, ties without shirts, glasses put on over masks or hats—if they want to hear their kids guffaw. Also, be prepared to repeat things. Young children might want you to make a fork fall off the table a good ten to twelve times before their laughter starts to slow down.

As kids get into kindergarten age, they start to like to misname objects, use "taboo" words, and make up nonsense words or funny rhymes. They love Dr. Seuss books because this is exactly what he does. *Fox in Socks, The Cat in the Hat,* and *Oh, the Thinks You Can Think* all fit this pattern. Through the middle grades of elementary school, riddles get popular, as do jokes—especially the knock-knock variety. Junior high or middle school often sees an end to childish humor. Kids still like to be silly, but they may worry that it is not "cool." Humor comes more from stories, and from put-downs, which are used by kids to help them figure out who they are, who they aren't, and who is like them and who is not. Finding fault in others is a major hobby at this age level, and our culture encourages it in our sitcoms and commercials. Try to expose kids to different kinds of humor. Bill Cosby and some of the old-time comics, like Lucille Ball, Sid Caesar, Dick Van Dyke, and Groucho Marx have great appeal to kids, especially through their television shows. You might be surprised to know how many early adolescents still like to sneak some peeks at *Happy Days* reruns—as well as at *The Muppet Show!* Parents also should know that, as kids feel better about themselves and more accepted, put-down humor will decrease, though, given our media, it is unrealistic to expect it to disappear completely.

HOUSEHOLD HUMOR BREAKS:
VITAMINS FOR POSITIVE ACTION

Think about the things you do that put a smile on your face or give you a warm, happy feeling. Some examples might include listening to music, reading, watching an old movie, listening to a favorite radio program, looking at old family pictures, sitting in a favorite chair, taking a moment to reflect on things, engaging in religious or spiritual observance, talking to cheerful people, taking a walk, or looking up at the clear night sky. Then take a careful look at how much time you spend in a typical day or a typical week doing these things. You probably will find that it is less time than you might have guessed.

To keep yourself in an optimistic frame of mind, try to do some things that put you in good humor every day, even if only for a short time—if not every day, then as often as you can. These small daily "humor breaks" are like powerful vitamins to build up and sustain your capacity to respond positively to parenting and other life challenges. As your children experience these moments, and as you share them as a family, you may find improvements in people's willingness to tolerate each other, deal with disappointments, and give each other the benefit of the doubt. A growing number of researchers are studying the benefits of an optimistic attitude and a life with regular doses of laughter and happiness. Among those who have written books for the general reader are Martin E. P. Seligman, *The Optimistic Child* (Houghton Mifflin, 1995); C. R. Snyder, *The Psychology of Hope: You Can Get There from Here* (Simon and Schuster, 1994); David G. Myers, *The Pursuit of Happiness* (William Morrow, 1992); and Mihaly Csikszentmihalyi, *Flow: The Psychology of Optimal Experience* (Harper & Row, 1990). Their consensus is that frequent humor breaks are even more valuable than highly intense but rare happy moments.

Here are some suggestions.

Find time to watch funny things together, things that everyone will enjoy. Unfortunately, this may tend to mean "classics," and not most of what is available now. Bill Cosby is a great family humorist. His early records (yes, he existed in the Vinyl Era) and videos of *The Bill Cosby Show* are classics. TV and cable stations broadcast reruns of Dick Van Dyke, Mary Tyler Moore, and *The Munsters*.

Write down three things that happened today that you feel good about. These can be small things: the shining of the sun, seeing a butterfly, getting a compliment, being on a winning team. Do this twice a week, maybe three times. Keep track of it, and be sure everyone shares what has been written. Don't judge what anyone else says. If it makes them feel good, that's what's important—as long as it's not something illegal or dangerous, of course.

The value of such a list is that it is available for sharing and review. When someone is down, it is a place to look for cheering up. It also makes the subtle point that we can create at least some of our happiness, we are not doomed to despair.

Try other things involving humor too, including the following.

A BOX OF HUGS

Emotionally Intelligent Parenting takes many forms! You actually may want to introduce something like this on Valentine's Day, or fathers can make this with their kids as a terrific Mother's Day present that will last a lifetime. (Moms, you could make this for Father's Day, but since mothers usually have lots of great ideas for Father's Day gifts, and fathers could almost always use some help in this area, please leave this for the dads, okay?)

Find a small box, like an empty "wipes" box or an index-card box. Put in it statements on index cards that, as in a game, entitle the person who picks a card to get a certain type and/or number of hugs. Why hugs? Hugs heal. Hugs help keep a family together.

Hugs are a safe way of sharing warm feelings, and are expressions of emotional intelligence without words. Here are some examples of Hug Cards:

A Hug and a Cookie (first comes the hug, then you share a favorite cookie)

A Mommy Hug

A Daddy Hug

A Kid Hug (which could involve one sibling hugging another)

A Sandwich Hug (two people do the hugging)

A Club Sandwich Hug (where the person who picks the card is in the middle, and everybody else gathers around to give the hug)

A Hug and a Bump (Remember the dance called the Bump? After you give a hug, you give a hip-to-hip "bump" on each side.)

A Hug and a Hum (while giving a hug, the person hums a song)

A Hug and a Hymn

A Hug and a Prayer (or blessing, or other positive saying or wish)

A Double Hug

A Triple Hug

A Hug and a Hop (hop together while hugging)

A High-Five Hug

A Low-Five Hug

A Sitting Hug

A No-Hands Hug

A No-Touch-but-Get-as-Close-as-You-Can Hug

A Big Hug

A Little Hug

A Loud Hug

A Foreign Hug (use your imagination!)

A Hug and a Buzz (make a buzzing sound during the hug)

A Hug and a Mug (after the hug, make for the person who

picked the card, or share together, a cup of coffee, tea, hot
chocolate, apple cider, or warm milk)
A Hug of Your Choice
A Few Hugs of Your Choice

You get the idea. Use these, add your own, and make changes
every once in a while to keep the idea fresh. If it is being given as
a present, the Hug Box can be decorated with permanent marker,
paints, stickers—anything that won't smudge off. (If you love
your mom, don't use glitter.) Parents, you might find yourselves
using this even when your kids are not around or involved. We
take no responsibility for the consequences, but if they are good,
you can give us a little credit!

WHAT WOULD _____ SAY OR DO?

When your child gets "stuck" and can't seem to figure out how to
handle a challenge—whether interpersonal or academic—you
can show that you care by asking how some character from
books, television, videos, or movies would handle it. Try to pick
a comical character from time to time. Since most kids have
watched *Sesame Street, Mister Rogers' Neighborhood,* or *Barney,* these are
still fun to ask about, even with high-school-aged children. Here
are some others we have used:

What would Sherman Potter have done? How about Bill Par-
cells? Sinbad? John Leguizamo? The Third Rock crowd? What
would Mary Richards have done? How about Batman or Robin?
Shari Lewis and Lamb Chop? Anybody from *Seinfeld?* How about
Hillary Clinton or Barbara Bush or Sarah Jordan or Ruth Bader
Ginsberg or Sandra Day O'Connor? Soupy Sales? White Fang
and Black Tooth? Kukla? Buffalo Bob? Julia Child? LeVar Burton?
Steve Martin? Paula Poundstone? Jesse Jackson? Engineer Scott?
The Holographic Doctor on *Star Trek Voyager?* Commander Data?
Tommy Lasorda? Curly Joe? The Road Runner? Fozzie Bear? Car-

los Santana? Mark Messier? Wayne Gretzky? William Safire? Barbara Walters? A host of ESPN's *Sports Center?* Jim Lehrer? Michael Eisner? Steven Spielberg? Obi-wan Kenobi? Si Hyung Lee? Kofi Annan? We are sure there are many others you might add to the list, depending on where you live and what you and your children enjoy.

Of course, it's good to take an occasional opportunity to educate your kids a bit if they don't know certain people, but you will be more effective if you tap into what they do know. For example, you can link your questions to books they are reading in school or people they are studying in history or science.

OTHER IDEAS

Set Chores to Music
Have special music that goes along with doing certain chores. Let the kids pick it out, or do it together. There is music to vacuum by, to do the dishes by, to remove the trash by, to fold the laundry by, to clean up the table by, and so on. Of course, when you put the music on, it signals that it is time for the task—this is a lot more pleasant, and more effective, than the usual parental nagging and reminder systems. It helps when the adults in the house do it first, when they are doing some chores. Feel free to sing along, dance around—have fun with it!!

Bring Chores to Life
Here are several examples:

Dear Billy,
I missed you yesterday. I was so full, I was hoping that you would take me to the sidewalk so that I could be emptied out, have my freedom, but no, it was not to be. Four more days of holding the family garbage. I would be lying if I said I was happy. I am not. Not only is it uncomfortable, but it is

smelly. I don't know what your parents cooked for dinner this week, but I just hope you did not have to eat it. I hope I will see you on Friday. Look for me by the back door.

Your friend, the Black Garbage Can

Hello, Sima. This is your blue jeans. I am leaving this telephone message because I want you to know I am sad. Sad because I do not think you care about me and my friends. We are your shirts and pants. We have been left out for two days now. We are not comfortable. We get hot, we get cold. Some of us would like to be in the drawer. Others of us really need to be hung up—we are getting muscle cramps from being folded. I was elected by the others to ask that you take care of us. Don't we take care of you? Thank you, and have a nice day.

We're not through:

To: Jess

From: dishes@sink.com

Dear Jess: I am a plate. I have food stuck to me and it is yucky. I understand from looking at the list on the refrigerator that you are supposed to clean me and my friends off after dinner. Well, this has not happened yet, and we are getting crusty. That will make us harder to clean, and much more unhappy. Please try to get to us very soon. What's that noise? Oh my—that's Cary Glass. The milk in him is starting to curdle. Call the Emergency Sponge! I have to go. Please come soon—the situation is getting serious.

You get the idea. Having a household that is not always solemn helps make it a place kids want to be. And parents you can laugh with are also parents you can approach when times are tough.

A FINAL WORD

Being a family—in the best sense of what that word means to you—is involved and not simple. Is it worth the effort? Yes. You will be surprised how much more meaning and fulfillment—and fun—you will find in your everyday life. Stick with it. Your kids probably won't thank you, at least until they are adults. But be assured that, deep down, on an EQ level, they will feel better, more regulated, more harmonious, because a proper balance in their lives will be restored, with their household as a safe haven, a source of caring, support, problem-solving assistance, and laughter. In our clinical cases, we see what happens when this is missing, in ways that parents often cannot see clearly or don't have access to. It is for this reason that some of our ancient sages stated that *Shalom Bayit*—the peace of the house—was one of the most important values one could uphold. They said this justifies parents being indirect, not always directly telling children about their shortcomings, and not always saying exactly how they might be feeling about what their children are doing.

The head and the heart both must be used in Emotionally Intelligent Parenting. Of course, some households are a little easier to manage than others. When there are difficulties, when children need a little extra help with managing their routines, the issue is perhaps one of children's skills. In the following chapter, we share some ways that parents can firmly but effectively help children to improve their self-control and express strong feelings.

Chapter 3

❦ How to Talk So Your Children Will THINK

■　■　■

As we have been emphasizing, teaching social competence and emotional intelligence requires a somewhat different approach to parenting. The emphasis is on getting children to think for themselves rather than on telling them what to do. This can be difficult for parents, because it does not come naturally. As parents, we want our children to become more perfect versions of ourselves. Also, because we love them, we want to spare them all the pain and heartache we experienced as a result of our mistakes. Therefore, we tend to tell them what to do based on our years of trial and error. However, the children probably will not listen in any case, and our job as parents is to teach children how to be independent in solving their own problems. We cannot always be there to tell them what to do and how they should behave, nor do we really want to. The goal of parenting is to teach children how to think for themselves and behave within a set of moral guidelines imparted by their parents.

Another thing that makes parenting so challenging is that it is impossible to be objective with your children. You are intensely emotionally bonded, and the nature of the relationship causes you to react to your child in an emotional manner rather than a cognitive one. When the child screams, "I hate you!" the parent does not think, "I see my child is frustrated and is externalizing this negative emotion toward me because I represent a safe target." Rather, the parent reacts to his or her own hurt, which introduces strong emotions into what would ideally be a more rational assessment of the situation and thoughtful action. Such high emotional intensity can lead parents to respond instinctively, throwing them back on whatever long-standing patterns were established in their childhoods. The resentment parents often feel as a result of reverting to such emotion-driven reactions creates anger, including sometimes misplaced anger at the child as the "cause" of all the problems, and this sets up the potential for a cycle of unpleasant, ineffective parent-child interactions.

So, when teaching emotional intelligence and social competence, your parental role is not to solve the child's problem or to make the child's decision, even though you want to. You need to step back and act as facilitator of the child's thinking and problem-solving. You need to separate yourself emotionally from the child's problem at this time. In this role, you are not the expert or savior imparting wisdom to your child, offering the perfect solution.

Emotional Intelligence Principles Highlighted in This Chapter's Activities

1. Be Aware of One's Own Feelings and Those of Others
☞ 2. Show Empathy and Understand Others' Points of View
☞ 3. Regulate and Cope Positively with Emotional and Behavioral Impulses
4. Be Positive Goal- and Plan-Oriented
☞ 5. Use Positive Social Skills in Handling Relationships

Skillful guidance through social decision-making can help children see that inappropriate behaviors do not in fact get them what they really want, which is most importantly love and acceptance. This is a principle of emotional intelligence that is more complex than it might seem at first. We live in an increasingly impulsive time; we want to be reachable at all times by phone, pager, and E-mail. We want our computers to be as fast as possible. Too many people have megahertz overdoses. The news is filled with examples of hostile takeovers and crimes that appear to result in little or no punishment. Getting children to think through what they want and resist impulses to act on strong feelings or wants that are unduly influenced by media and peer pressure is a challenge that requires constant parental vigilance.

What can parents do that will help their children learn to think and problem-solve effectively? Our experiences as parents, psychologists, clinicians, researchers, and practitioners have taught us a set of EQ Guiding Principles for putting emotional intelligence into action. Most of us, however, have been taught another set of principles that have led to long-term problems for parents and children:

How to Talk So Your Children Will <u>Not</u> Think

1. Tell them exactly what you think all the time.

2. Evaluate their ideas or statements as soon as they make them. Label them as "good" or "bad."

3. Every chance you get, give them wisdom from your own childhood ("When I was your age...").

4. Eliminate any chance of disappointment by preventing children from going down a path you think will not work. "There's no way that can happen." "No smart person would even think about things like that."

5. Be very serious at all times. Homework, chores, taking care of siblings, extracurricular activities, and sports are responsibilities that need to be treated in a solemn, dignified, and stoic manner.

6. Say less rather than more. There is no need to repeat oneself much, if at all. Explanations should be given once. Children need to listen carefully the first time, and besides, they know what adults mean.

7. "Do as I say, not as I do."

8. Present yourself as perfect. Never show your children that you do not understand or that you are wrong.

These instructions embody some conventional wisdom handed down from earlier generations of parenting, and some ideas that seem to persist from decade to decade. Some of these ideas are associated with certain cultural backgrounds. There is no point in looking at them as "right" or "wrong" in any absolute sense. But we do have to ask how suitable they are for the current era in which we are raising our children and for the upcoming times when our children have to function as adults. In our view, anything more than the infrequent use of these principles can lead to trouble.

When used extensively by parents, each of these "anti-principles" erects roadblocks in children's thinking processes. They do so in different ways—some by not giving children information they need; others by cutting out possibilities even from consideration. Some reflect uncertainty about exactly what it is that parents should do to get their points across to children. Others treat children as miniature adults, which they certainly are not.

Parents need to build relationships with their children so that they can guide and teach them. There are too many competing influences on children now for parents to assume that simply because they are parents, they should and will be obeyed. For better or worse, we live in an Age of Questioning. And the key to responding to children's questions is not to jump in with an answer. The key is to lecture less and listen more; to tell less and show more; to direct less and question more; to substitute internal persuasion for parental coercion; to build character from the inside out, not to demand it. This cannot happen unless a relationship has been established between parents and children, and both are emotionally intelligent, thinking and caring partners in that relationship.

The reason for setting out our set of guiding principles is that they are a family's strongest antidote against the impulse to act without thinking and caring. They are based on the belief that Emotionally Intelligent Parenting is directed toward helping children acquire the skills they need for emotionally intelligent living. The word *skills* means that learning must take place, with all the trial and error that this implies. You are guiding and facilitating, rather than pontificating or demanding.

This can make parents uncomfortable if it is perceived as a loss of control or an abdication of authority. But this is not the case. The parent guides the child through a process, but must be willing to give up preconceived notions of what the "right" answer is. This, like our negative guidelines, will only stifle the child's thinking. When children are resistant and parents try to lead them to the "right" answer, parents are very likely to end up frustrated, with an argument not far behind.

Let's not think, however, that things are necessarily better if a child is compliant. Indeed, cooperation may be a way of giving parents what they want to hear. But that says little about what the child actually thinks and feels, and what the child might do when a situation arises. To tell a child what do to in any given situation and have the child follow that directive is not the same as teaching children to problem-solve on their own, when there are no adults around and the pressure—from peers or other influences—is on.

We want to reassure you that problem-solving does not occur in a values vacuum. While parents encourage their children to think for themselves, they certainly have the responsibility to establish a moral framework. Skillful guidance through the problem-solving process helps children think about their behavior through those values, to serve as a benchmark for helping children set their own goals for themselves.

For example, when a child says that her goal is to drop out of school, the parent should not immediately reprimand, punish, or lecture the child on the value of education. (By the way, adolescents will often bait parents with this kind of purposeful rejection of parental values in their attempt to establish their own identities. Don't worry, it's usually temporary, unless you reinforce them by arguing about it.) Technically, what the parent should do is clarify to the child that dropping out of school is something he can do to achieve a goal, but it is not really a goal in itself. If the child's goal is to have fun, then the parent should help her think of other things she can also do to achieve this. Then, when the child is thinking about the potential consequences of her actions, the parent can ask what might happen if she drops out of school. If the child has not already thought of it, the parent can help her envision working long hours for low pay and not having time or money for fun.

It is important for parents to talk not just so that kids will listen and obey, but so that they will think and reflect on the values that the family believes are important (as we recommend establishing in chapter 2). The parent who takes time to help the child think through negative scenarios rather than immediately reprimanding him will be helping the child build skills to use when he has to make tough decisions on his own, without parents around to guide him.

The EQ Guiding Principles for helping our children to think are organized into three groups: Everyday Principles, Questioning Techniques, and Tips for the Long Term. They are also ranked from easiest to most difficult. Please be patient with yourself in learning how to do them. (This may also help give you added empathy for the difficulties your children experience when they have to master a new and difficult skill.)

The EQ Guiding Principles

Everyday Principles
1. Modeling
2. Prompting and cuing previously learned skills
3. Paraphrasing

Questioning Techniques
4. Open-ended questioning
5. The two-question rule
6. The Columbo technique

Tips for the Long Term
7. Patience and persistence
8. Flexibility and creativity
9. Developmental adaptation

EVERYDAY PRINCIPLES

Our everyday routines and interactions with family members provide many of the best opportunities for emotionally intelligent parenting. Truly, these are the best times. They happen often, they don't require massive changes on parents' parts, and yet, through repetition, they can make a very big difference to your household and how it functions, in the time and energy (and grief) spent on regular routines, and in the skills for everyday living that your children develop.

1. Modeling
Modeling allows a child to learn by watching adults use skills, and allows parents to teach by example, which is much more effective than just telling the child what to do. It is unfortunate that often adults do not let children in on their thought

processes. Letting children in on the adult's thoughts can let them know that it is normal to have negative feelings, be confused, and not have the perfect solution right at their fingertips. It shows children that you can think your way out of a problem. Of course, parents need to model the self-control and good communication skills they expect of the child as well.

One mother we worked with remarked casually that her child called her stupid. When the therapist indicated that this was not acceptable, the father offered that the mother called the child stupid all the time. This was obviously not helpful, but under the circumstances it was understandable, given the mother's degree of frustration and lack of other ways of handling her child's behavior. Nevertheless, if the mother's goal was to change her child's behavior, she would first have to change her own.

Poor modeling poses this challenge for parents: we want our kids to change, but will we change? Who should be expected to change first—an adult or a child? Logic would suggest the adult, who should have the wisdom, skills, perspective, discipline, and self-control to change. But we all know better, don't we? It is not easy to change. Old patterns are hard to give up. It takes work, reminders, and the patient assistance of those around us.

It is no different for our kids, especially when they are not clear about the great benefits a new behavior will bring. For example, we worked with a child whose study habits were awful. Reading was done with a Walkman plugged into his head; papers were kept in haphazard piles; his eyes would get tired fairly quickly— possibly because he liked to work with relatively little illumination. Test performance beginning in ninth grade was miserable, although there had been no problems before that time. Parents and teachers were at their wits' end; the child didn't see what all the fuss was about.

We asked the child to tell us how he studied, and then we asked how he learned to do this. His answer: from his dad. The child told stories his dad had related about college, and the child also discussed how his dad sometimes worked in the family room with the TV on, all his papers scattered about, a cup of coffee in one hand and the phone in the other. Quite a talented father!

When we brought this information to the father, he reflected for a moment, then agreed that the parallels between his own and his son's study habits were strong. But, he said, he worked well and efficiently. Then we asked if he used the same strategies throughout his elementary-school career and into high school. His reply: "Of course not. I started working this way when I got to college." The father then realized that his son learned from his current modeling and not from previous behaviors that were perhaps more germane for the child.

Dad got the idea: his was an example of poor modeling. What he was showing the child in the present was not what his child needed to see. As things turned out, Dad did not need to radically change his current approach. He had to have a talk with his son about how he studied in the past, and we worked with him to patiently guide and correct his son. Once Dad shared what he used to do (which was validated by a grandparent and an uncle, at our urging), the entire interaction around studying changed. There was less struggle, bitterness, and anger. Dad also watched himself a little better, working with adequate light and turning off the television.

2. Prompting and cuing previously learned skills

It is not enough just to teach skills; they need to be practiced in the real world. One way to get children to use skills more independently and spontaneously is to remind them. Now, there is a difference between a reminder and nagging. *Nagging* is associated with words like *carping, criticizing, scolding, flaying*—most unpleasant. *Nudge* is associated with words like *drive, propel, shove, push*—a little better. *Remind* is associated with *suggest, cue, stir, jog*. There is a critical difference. Reminders give credit to the individual for having a mind. What the adult is doing is helping the mind to focus. Nudging is the same basic idea, but implies that the mind needs a lot more help. Nagging suggests a defective mind, that failure to do whatever was supposed to be done is "wrong." Is it any wonder that children (and spouses?) develop an "off" switch when nagging starts—or at least healthy ones do.

There are some specific ways to remind, or even nudge, effectively. It is helpful to use a prompt or a simple way of indicating to the child that now would be a good time to use the skills they have learned previously. Let's take an example from dinner. In many households, children are used to *Star Trek* technology. What do we mean? Dinner is "beamed" to the table and then, after dinner, the leftovers, dishes, and so on are dematerialized.

How do we know this? Children typically appear at the dinner table seconds before the food is served and are themselves "beamed away" right after, or during, the consumption of the final bite of the meal. Or so it looks to us. Parental intervention at both ends of the event go something like this:

"Well, go ahead and sit down. Why don't you help?"

"Nobody asked me to."

"I have to ask? Every night we go through this same conversation. I have to ask? You should *know*. Next time, I want you to help out!"

"Okay."

After the meal:

"That was good. [Note: Kids rarely say this, but we wanted to have *some* dialogue!] Bye."

"Where are you going? What about the dishes? Put away the milk. And don't forget to clear your plate."

Sometimes this will bring a child back. But not usually.

"Next time I will. I have to call Pat now." [A more emotionally intelligent child will at least say something like, "I have to listen to National Public Radio" or "I have to study. You don't want me to fail my test, do you?"]

The parent is left with few good choices. This situation is beyond reminders. Nagging is likely to occur.

How do we *prompt* help? First we define what we mean. There will be two prompts: helping out with dinner and cleaning up after dinner. You can define helping out however you like, appropriate for children (and spouses?—remember the first guideline!) of toddler age and older. "At dinnertime, I want you to help out. That means you are going to set the table [or take out beverages, fold napkins, stir the vegetables, whatever makes sense to arrange in advance that your child can do]." Of course, as they get older, you can teach them more and more skills to help out in more and more ways.

Cleaning up works similarly. Here is another format: "After dinner, I would like you to help clean up. Which job would you like to do this week?" Once this is set, parents now have a prompt to use. Why? Because children are unlikely to remember to follow through. Either they will forget or, because they are used to being nudged and nagged, wait for that to come. If it doesn't come beforehand, then fine, they won't have to do anything. If it comes afterwards—hey, we can just tune it out.

Prompts are reminders—they "jog," and they do so in advance. *Before* dinner, the parent says, "I want you to help out with dinner in ten minutes." This is no longer an ambiguous statement. It means that a specific thing needs to be done in a specific time frame. It is a reminder of a previous conversation. And it will take a few reminders—or maybe more than a few—before you might expect a voluntary action. *After* dinner, the prompt is, "Remember to clean up before you get started with anything else." If it involves something that can't be done until others completely finish their coffee or tea, you might add, "I will call you when everyone is done—figure about ten minutes, so don't go on-line or anything you can't interrupt."

By using a simple prompt, parents do not have to stop the action and review a whole set of skills or sequence of activities. In addition, a prompt to use a skill is much different from a criticism. Teaching a child who speaks too loudly and quickly some specific ways to speak more quietly and slowly (such as by opening her mouth less widely, breathing between sentences, and remembering her "quiet voice") can be paired with the prompt to "quiet down." Saying to a child, "Honey, now would be a good time to use 'quiet down,'" will be perceived a lot differently than "Would you just quiet down?" even though both mean the same thing to the parent.

Your mind is probably already racing ahead to 150 times during the day when you want to use prompts. Let us urge you to resist. Pick a couple of places to start—as at dinnertime, or during morning or bedtime routines—and put those in place consistently. Once you find that the prompts are understood and have become fairly routine, then you can begin to add them to other areas. Just try to be patient—it will pay off.

For many children, it is helpful when others in the children's environment are taught the same prompts and when to use them. Indeed, there are some schools in which prompts are taught and then conveyed to parents, so they can follow through and use them. (We refer you to M. Elias, J. Zins, R. Weissberg, et al., *Promoting Social and Emotional Learning: Guidelines for Educators*, Alexandria, Va.: Association for Supervision and Curriculum Development, 1997.) In other cases, prompts that parents find successful are explained to the school and adapted for use there. Generally speaking, the more pervasive the prompting of skills, the quicker the child will learn. In schools, teachers and even lunch aides can be taught to use prompts rather than nagging and yelling at students to sit down and shut up. The prompting of a skill instead of attempting to gain obedience through invective can be a more positive and effective intervention.

As you probably can tell, using prompts with your children helps them build some important skills related to their self-control and self-discipline. Prompts that are useful to help children calm down when they are starting to get upset, and to remind them how to behave appropriately with others, are "Keep Calm" and "Be your BEST." "Keep Calm" is a relaxation exercise that can be used anywhere and anytime when children need to settle down from an overstimulating experience or when they are feeling an overwhelming emotion. We will describe these in detail in chapter 5.

3. Paraphrasing

To paraphrase is to reword, restate, summarize, or repeat what someone else has just said. To put it another way, paraphrasing involves taking what was said and putting it another way, to make sure you understood what the speaker meant to convey, and to let the speaker know that he or she was clear. Should we paraphrase this again? We will spare you. However, this strategy should be familiar to anyone who has had training in communication skills, management or supervision, or experience with marriage counseling.

Paraphrasing is important because it helps the other person feel acknowledged and understood. By reflecting back to someone what he or she is saying, you let the person know that you are taking them seriously and that the feelings and thoughts that were expressed are important. By repeating your child's words, you are making sure you really know what he or she is saying, and you are letting your child know that you understand.

Another useful aspect of paraphrasing is that the parent can gently rephrase the child's statements into more accurate or appropriate language. Children often have difficulty stating their feelings. For example, when asked how they feel, a child might respond, "He's an idiot." This can be paraphrased, "It sounds like you are really angry with him." It is often necessary to translate the child's rough expression of feelings into more refined and precise statements. This will help children clarify their own thoughts and feelings as well as develop a better problem-solving vocabulary.

Here is a somewhat extreme example. You might try something like it yourself for fun when you are on the phone with your spouse or an in-law, or one of those sales calls that disrupts your dinner.

WIFE: Hi, honey.
HUSBAND: You are opening the conversation with a greeting.
WIFE: Ahh, yes...I wanted to know how you were and what happened with the kids today.

HUSBAND: You are showing concern with the state of my health and with the well-being of our progeny. You are relating in a caring way.

WIFE: Are you okay? Did something happen? Are there robbers in the house? Have you been abducted by aliens?

HUSBAND: Hearing some unexpected responses from me has aroused a sense of concern in you. You appear to be looking for an explanation.

WIFE: Is this some kind of game? Is your mother there? I really don't appreciate this kind of thing. What's with you? Here I am trying to have a normal conversation, and you...

In the example above, the final statement indicates that this is a good time, or just past it, to explain that you are practicing paraphrasing. Just remember, too much paraphrasing without some actual responding can get people quite annoyed. This may be good or bad, depending on whom you are talking to.

QUESTIONING TECHNIQUES

If there is a common thread running through the questioning techniques we recommend, it is that they operate through a facilitative approach, that is, they involve teaching by asking questions rather than telling. Also inherent in this approach is a non-authoritarian manner. It is necessary to lead, or even at times to push, children to think through decisions and choices with a strategy: figure out their feelings, put their problems into words, set their own goals, and decide their own course of action. This is a lot better than parents' steering kids toward what the parents always believe to be best, or even toward what parents may think their child should want.

4. Open-ended questioning

There are four types of questioning:

- *Causal questioning:* "Why did you hit him?"; "Why can't you remember what I tell you?"; "Why won't you help your sister?"
- *Multiple-choice questioning:* "Did you hit him because he was teasing you, because he took something from you, or because you were angry about something else?"; "Do you remember things when I yell them, when I say them fifty times, or when I leave notes all over your room?"; "Will you help your sister if I scream, if I offer you a reward, or do I have to threaten you?"
- *True-false questioning:* "Did you hit him, yes or no?"; "Can't you remember things when I tell you?"; "Will you help your sister or not?"
- *Open-ended questioning:* "What happened between the two of you?"; "What could I do that will make it easier for you to remember the important things I ask you to do?"; "How can we figure out a way for you to help your sister when she needs it?"

Most children have difficulty answering "why" questions, because there is often an underlying accusation, and children, like most adults, become defensive when they feel blamed. Moreover, most adults ask "why" questions in problem situations. As you know, most children say "I don't know" or "I didn't do it" in response to a "why" question.

In truth, if we could do a mental CAT scan, we would see that an accurate answer to a "why" question is impossible without recognizing and acknowledging the child's own weakness in emotional intelligence skills. Such a scan would reveal that, in response to the question "Why did you hit him?" a child would accurately say, "Because I have poor emotional control and tend to act impulsively rather than consider alternative actions that may be more effective in solving the problem in the long run." If only such insights were forthcoming from other adults, let alone children!

Now, we don't ever expect that any of us will give up cause-seeking, true-false, and multiple-choice questions. And there are times when such questions are useful. But parents need to be sure that there is a better balance of open-ended questions in their conversations with their children. This is similar to the four basic food groups: a good diet requires a daily balance. Treat causal questions like high-fat and high-cholesterol foods, and you will keep the family arteries of communication free from blockages.

To do this requires most parents to retrain themselves to ask more open-ended questions. A good first step is to practice ways of reframing "why" questions. Here are some examples:

"What happened?"
"What did you want to happen?"
"How are you feeling?"
"What was the other person doing?"
"What happened before this?"

Parents are often too quick to give multiple-choice questions, especially if children tend to be resistant. Parents can usually make a good guess what the possibilities are, and present them in a succinct format. However, a goal of Emotionally Intelligent Parenting is to have the child become a competent thinker who can make up his mind clearly when adults are not available to help, even when there is peer pressure. This is much more likely to happen when children are encouraged to think for themselves from the start.

The exceptions to this are with younger children and when there are time constraints. Younger children will not always be able to say what they want to, or may not be able to put the right words to their ideas and feelings. They usually will need the prompts provided by multiple-choice questions, at least as a check against what they have said. Also, using only open-ended questions can be time-consuming, especially with resistant children. Therefore, while the rule of thumb is to start off with open-ended questions, multiple-choice questions can be considered first in some situations. It is also important to avoid asking questions that can be answered yes or no. If one asks, "Are you angry?" much less information will be elicited than if the question is phrased in an open-ended manner such as, "What feelings are you having?"

If the parent takes the role of supreme authority or censor, children will not feel encouraged to think and explore ideas, because they can never "lead" anywhere. Adolescents are especially wary of others telling them what to do. Children and adolescents will often bait adults with inappropriate responses, waiting patiently for the adult to bite, causing the discussion to stray from the topic or end up in an argument. By not setting yourself up as an unquestioned expert, there is less to rebel or argue against. Also, this makes you an ally of the child, rather than the "enemy." Open-ended questioning, although more time-consuming, creates a positive climate that will allow children to feel ownership of the solution.

5. The two-question rule

This simple but powerful rule comes to us through research in schools on the kinds of questions that seem to promote the most learning. The answer includes not only open-ended questions, but also the two-question rule. The rule is simple: "Follow up a question with another question." It reminds the parent to stay in the questioning mode. For example, "How are you feeling?" "Good." "What other feelings are you aware of?" "Well, I'm a little nervous." From here, we can move into some paraphrasing and then perhaps some more open-ended questions.

How does the two-question rule work? Think about times you were in school, perhaps sitting in a circle or in rows, and the teacher asked a question that everyone was going to have to answer. What did you do? Most kids think about their answer over and over, so they will be ready to say it when their turn comes. After their turn, they sigh in relief. They really have not listened to much of what came before or after their turn.

Ah, but the two-question rule changes a lot of that. Notice:

"What are the different parts of the rain forest?" "The canopy." "Good! Where is the canopy and how tall is it?" Let's do another one of those mental CAT scans: "Whoa! You mean I have to *think*?" the kid says to himself. "What did I say, anyway? Canopy. What did other people say? Oh, why didn't I listen? Sammy Smart-guy said something about the trees and how tall they are...what was it? Arrggh!" As this mental activity is going on, the other students observe a child in shock that a follow-up question was asked. Here is a mental CAT scan of another student: "Wow. I was going to say 'animals that are almost extinct.' But what if she asks me for an example? Let me think—no, let me look it up. Ah—butterflies. Whew. Now I'm ready." And another: "Man, am I lucky she didn't ask me something. I said something about slashing and burning forests, but that was on Rudy's paper—I have no idea what it means. Next time, I better pay attention!"

Not only does more information come forth, it requires kids to think at a deeper level than they otherwise might. Here is an example from a household: "What did you do in social studies today?" "We talked about World War I." "Oh. What about it did you discuss?" "Huh?" "What about it did you discuss—how or why it started, who was in it, how it went, where it took place, what happened?" "Uhh, it was, uhh, how it started." "Was that the war where someone was killed and that started things off?" "Yeah, it was an Arch-Deluxe Ford Expedition or something like that." "Hmm, maybe the Archduke Ferdinand?" "Yeah. That's it." "What did your teacher say about whether or not this was the real reason the war started?" "Uhh, I'm not sure. We have to read more in the book for homework." "Okay, I'd like to look it over with you when you are finished. This is stuff I remember learning, but it would be fun for me to refresh my memory a bit—you know how I forget things!"

The more the child talks about the problem or situation, the more understanding both the parent and child will have. Of course, there are applications with friends and, of course, with siblings. "Such crying, such screaming! Myrtle, what happened?"

"She called me a name." "Willow called you a name? What name?" "It was a bad name, a curse name." "Really! Well! What was it?" "It was, uh, mean." "It was a mean name, or she called you mean?" "She called me mean." "Myrtle, you know that is not a curse, though it is not a nice thing to be called. Willow, what happened before I came in?" "She ruined my game." "She did? How? What did she do?" "She tried to take my cars." "You mean she came up and grabbed your cars?" "Yes. No. She asked me for them all." "And then she grabbed them?" "Yes. No." "Was it yes or no? Did she grab the cars or touch the cars?" "No." "What did you say?" "I said, 'Go away.'" "And what happened next?" "I said she was mean. And she said I am not. And I said she was." "Well, now I think I understand. You both said things that did not quite happen. Willow did not curse at you. And Myrtle did not ruin your game. When she asked you nicely, how could you have answered so she would not have gotten upset at you?" "Just said no?" "Myrtle, would that have helped?" "Yes." "And what could you have done so that Willow would not have gotten so upset at you?" "Not asked for all her cars." "Young ladies, I am proud of both of you. Next time, remember, I will ask you about what really happened, so you can save us a lot of time when you tell a story by telling it exactly like there was a video camera in the room getting it all on videotape."

Follow-up questioning, especially combined with the other guiding principles, helps children clarify their own thoughts and feelings, learn to be more clear, and help parents get a line on what actually is going on. But, as with paraphrasing, there is an art to knowing when and how much to persist. That's why it's a two-question rule and not a four-question rule. Generally, two questions in a row work the best.

6. The Columbo technique

This strategy was modeled after the television detective Lieutenant Columbo. This character feigns confusion and asks lots of questions in an offhand manner. He scratches his head and has difficulty understanding. He is nonthreatening, and therefore the people he is questioning do not get defensive. By pointing out inconsistencies in witnesses' stories or having suspects explain the obvious, he obtains the crucial information to solve the case.

This strategy is particularly effective when working with resistant children. For example, if two siblings were in a fight and one claims that the other hit him for no reason, the parent might ask, "You mean he just came up and hit you? Gee, that's strange. Where were you? Show me. Ah. And he came from where? There? Not there? Oh, maybe there? Well, anyway, what did you say to him before he hit you?" And so on. Through this line of questioning, you are never directly challenging the child's statements. Instead, you let inconsistencies come out, or keep getting enough information in a roundabout way to get the child to verbalize what really happened.

The essential aspect of the Columbo technique is its nonconfrontational manner. It is important never to say something like "Come on, I know you are lying," even when you know that the truth has yet to be spoken. It is through gentle persistence that the truth will come out. After all, truth comes out when people feel it is safe or in their best interests to speak the truth.

This can be a time-consuming process, but when you as a parent do not know what is going on, it is often the best way to find out. With resistant children, the more the parent pushes, the more resistant the child becomes. With the Columbo technique, their oppositional nature often leads them to want to show you, the "stupid adult," what you do not know. Eventually, that can lead to showing you the truth.

TIPS FOR THE LONG TERM

Emotionally Intelligent Parenting is not a fad or a gimmick or a technique; it is a way of relating to your children and of organizing your household. You will not use all of the principles all of the time. You don't have to. You just have to use more of the princi-

ples more of the time, and your children—and you—will benefit. For this to happen, we have identified some Guiding Principles that work over the long term to support Emotionally
Intelligent Parenting.

7. Patience and persistence

As has been mentioned previously, helping children learn to
become effective problem-solvers and responsible, caring deci-
sion-makers takes a long time. It involves teaching a complex set
of skills. Although all children need to learn these skills, some are
more facile than others. Just as some children teach themselves to
read and others are dyslexic, some children develop these social
skills naturally or at least more easily in response to adult guidance, while others have difficulty reading social cues, compre-
hending interpersonal problems, and expressing themselves in a
manner that will enable them to have their needs met.

These children have what we call "social dyslexia." Just as a
child with reading dyslexia needs more time and effort devoted
to reading instruction, one with social dyslexia needs more time
and effort devoted to formal or informal instruction in the area of
social decision-making. Anyone who claims there is an easy way
or a short way to accomplish this is not being truthful. For children with social dyslexia, progress follows only from long and
hard work on these skills. But the good news is that progress does
follow. Since none of the birth certificates we have seen include
warranties for easy use, if kids require a lot, then we have to provide it.

Fortunately, this is a road that is well traveled, and it is one
with pathways to success. It is important that you be patient with
your children learning these skills, and also that you be patient
with yourself in learning some of these new ways of parenting.

Along with patience comes persistence. The more something
is taught at different times and from different perspectives, the
better chance there is that it will be internalized. Take the time to
listen to what your child is really trying to say, ask a question and

wait for an answer, and explain things to your child when he or she does not understand, even though it may take a while longer than you might have thought it would.

And be persistent over the years of your child's development. These techniques are not just for use with a particular age group. And, like the ideas of Dr. Haim G. Ginott, a leader in focusing on how parents should speak to their children to build better relationships with them, and those of T. Berry Brazelton, who is revered as one of the foremost pediatricians in America, the strategies in this book can be used for years and years. Most parents, after reading a book or attending a parenting workshop, are enthusiastic about what they have learned. But often these are "quick fixes," and, as time goes by, they do not apply, or they are too difficult to sustain, or parents forget the new strategy and revert to old patterns. If you need to reread parts of this book every six months or so, that is okay. It's not as if you will be starting a whole new approach every six months. In actuality, what we now know to be Emotionally Intelligent Parenting is the kind of practice that has been recognized as valuable for quite a while. Now we just know more about how parents must be patient and persistent in today's society if the message is to get through to children over the current media barrage.

8. *Flexibility and creativity*

We know how busy today's families are, and that in many ways families are too busy. We could tell you to slow down, program fewer activities for your children, find time for yourselves, stop and smell the roses, and spend an hour a day deliberately modeling and teaching social and emotional skills, but we know you will not do this (we don't do it, either). Therefore you need to be flexible and creative in how you do manage family life. As we will show you, you can work on these skills around the dinner table, while out shopping, standing in line for a movie, or driving your car, and when problems do arise, you have to take the time to deal with them. What we are suggesting is that you integrate the

Emotionally Intelligent Parenting approach into your regular lifestyle, rather than change your lifestyle dramatically. In order to do this, you need to be flexible.

A lot of what we know has been taught to us by the families we have worked with. We are observers and collectors. Families we have worked with have come up with their own techniques and activities through their own flexibility and creativity. The Guiding Principles enumerated in this chapter can be thought of as the raw ingredients from which creativity can emerge. This way, parents can be confident in what they are creating! We encourage you to come up with your own methods for Emotionally Intelligent Parenting. Once you understand the basic framework, it is all a matter of creative application. This also makes it more fun. And please send us your adaptations so that we can have material for our next book!

9. Developmental adaptation

This principle is a long-term tip that gives us additional reasons for flexibility and creativity and patience and persistence. Our parenting needs to grow as our children grow. And if we have more than one child, our parenting must adapt to the unique life situation of each child. Parents cannot treat all of their children the same because even when they are the same ages, they live in different eras. As parents, we are not the same people with our second or third eight-year-old as we were with our first. And that's good! Take advantage of what life has taught you!

A FINAL WORD

No parent follows all of the Guiding Principles all the time. Nor is this necessary. What we see, though, is that too many parents follow too few of the principles even a little. When this happens, kids suffer. We want to restore a better balance, a balance that helps children grow socially, emotionally, and intellectually. This happens by starting with the principles that you can follow and sticking with them, and gradually adding some others. By doing a few more small things more often, parents can make a big difference in the well-being of their children!

In the next chapter, we give parents some ideas for how to organize their households so that children can improve their self-control and self-discipline and there can be at least a little more household peace and organization.

Chapter 4

Self-Direction and Self-Improvement:
The EQ Approach to Discipline

■　　■　　■

PARENT (calmly): Please, Robbie, don't yell at your sister at the dinner table. If she didn't give you the potatoes when you asked for them, just ask her again.

PARENT (a few seconds later, less calmly, and a bit louder): Robbie, that tone of voice is still kind of loud. You have to ask in a nicer way!!

PARENT (thirty seconds later; face is bright red; veins in neck are visible and pulsating; hands are grasping the arms of the chair so tightly that the bones look like they are going to come through the skin; tone of voice is loud—very loud): ROBBIE! ENOUGH IS ENOUGH. DON'T YOU KNOW HOW TO TALK TO SOMEONE WITHOUT SCREAMING? YOU HAVE TO LEARN HOW TO CALM DOWN WHEN YOU DON'T GET YOUR WAY!!!!!

Hmm...

Though we know that you have never found yourself in the above situation, or at least not too often, not more than weekly or perhaps daily, we also know that you know people who have found themselves worked up like this parent.

There is something ironic about a parent yelling at a child to stop yelling or a parent hitting a child for hitting a sibling. We are not telling parents not to yell or not to hit their children. These are controversial issues for which research does not give clear guidance. But we certainly want you to think about what these behavior management and EQ-building techniques—and that's what they are—may be teaching your child inadvertently. The lesson may be that the way to get people to do what you want is to intimidate them. This may not be what parents really want to teach, even if it does seem to "work" at times.

Indeed, many parents use what we call "normal disciplining techniques." These usually consist of what their parents did to them, including such old standards as yelling, spanking, threatening, lecturing, taking things away, and other kinds of punishments. But again we ask, what is all this teaching a child? "You hit your brother, so no dessert." What does hitting have to do with food? Maybe the child should just time the hitting better, and beat the brother up after dessert.

Our children live in complicated times. This makes modeling that parents provide in discipline situations more important than we might think. In this chapter we review the four basic strategies that have been found by many parents to be more effective than "normal disciplining techniques" for all children, but especially for more challenging children. "Easy" children respond to almost anything, often not needing much more than "the look." (You know "the look"—usually one parent has it, and certain teachers also do; it freezes you in your tracks, and you feel waves of guilt about everything wrong you have ever done, even things the person could have no way of knowing about.) But we want to emphasize the "teaching" part of parenting strategies so that this will not get lost in an attempt to "manage" or "control" immediate or disruptive, disobedient behaviors. Our four strategies work to further develop all children's social awareness, emotional sensitivity, and self-direction. With more difficult children, you will need to use these techniques with greater consistency and patience.

Although these strategies are probably already familiar to you, there may be some subtle differences from how you may be using them or have heard about them. Much of this is a matter of attitude and purpose. The strategies are not punishments; they are tools to teach respect, responsibility, self-direction, self-awareness, and thoughtful compliance. The difference between disciplining, which means "to teach," and punishing, which means "to cause to undergo pain," is in how parents think about these techniques and the ways they are used.

Emotional Intelligence Principles Highlighted in This Chapter's Activities

☞ 1. Be Aware of One's Own Feelings and Those of Others
   2. Show Empathy and Understand Others' Points of View
☞ 3. Regulate and Cope Positively with Emotional and Behavioral Impulses
☞ 4. Be Positive Goal- and Plan-Oriented
   5. Use Positive Social Skills in Handling Relationships

The emotional intelligence principles involved help parents (a) become aware of their own feelings and those of their children, (b) use strategies that allow their kids to deal with their strong feelings and impulsive actions in positive, learning-oriented ways, and (c) keep focused on the goals of "teaching" rather than "punishing." A likely by-product of how the principles in this chapter are used is a reduced level of harsh conflict within the home. Why is this? Constructive, patient, family problem-solving and responsible decision-making by children are unlikely to take place in a home where children are out of control or where parents are viewed as despots. Harsh conflict sets up power struggles between parent and child. It creates "winners" and "losers," and invites attempts to get "revenge." In order to learn problem-solving, children must believe and feel that parents are "on their side." This involves a whole other set of values, such as "sincerity," "trust," and "openness." The discipline strategies in this chapter are intended to first and foremost improve the relationships among family members.

PRAISE AND PRIORITIZE

As humans, we are pre-wired to be social beings. We need one another. We need one another to fulfill our collective economic needs, and we need one another for love and companionship. We also need one another to cope with everyday life. Babies in orphanages die not from lack of food, shelter, and clothing, but from lack of voice, touch, and love. Everyone needs attention, human contact, and caring relationships. We find that the search for caring relationships and positive attention are primary motivators of behavior, especially for children. Often parents wonder, "Why would he be doing this for attention? I already spend an inordinate amount of time with him, and when he has a problem, the whole family seems to revolve around him. How much attention does this kid need?"

Attention is habit-forming, not just something we really like, such as a dessert. After a huge, lavish meal, no matter how enticing the dessert, you reach a point where you say, "Enough." But children rarely will say, "You know, Mom, you've paid enough attention to me today. I'm just going to play quietly by myself and let you get some work done." No, attention is habit-forming in children, and they are biologically designed to both want and like attention so much that they never seem to have enough. Of course, the more negative attention they receive, the more insecure they become, which leads them to try to get more attention. This cycle can become a problem, because negative attention is not nearly as satisfying as positive attention.

Children may not seem as if they care what kind of attention they are getting, positive or negative. That is why a parent may yell, but find that the child does not stop or soon does the inappropriate behavior again. Often parents ask the child, "Why do you make me yell at you?" The answer may be that the child wants you to pay attention to him. But the deeper answer is that children lack the emotional intelligence skills to get positive attention, or that their parents' "antennae" for children's positive attention-seeking behavior might need a little EQ adjustment.

Favorite ways in which parents give negative attention to kids:

> Lecture
>
> Nag
>
> Scold
>
> Yell

Which leads kids to:

> Tune parents out
>
> Hum
>
> Run away or avoid parents
>
> Do the same things again that got the negative attention

RESETTING YOUR POSITIVE ATTENTION ANTENNA

The model we use for giving attention to children is to give positive attention for appropriate behavior, and withdraw attention for annoying but harmless inappropriate behavior. When children misbehave, it is more common for parents to completely withdraw positive attention and to give negative attention for inappropriate behavior, in the form of parental nagging, scolding, lecturing, or yelling. As much as possible, the parent should reduce the amount of negative attention a child receives, as this tends to increase conflict within the home and lower the self-esteem of both parent and child. Why? Negative attention can be habit forming, and we do not think that any parent wants to set up a pattern whereby they have to yell at or nag their children to get them to do something. By understanding the principles that are operating, parents can have many more choices of ways to handle misbehavior.

Parents usually do not conceptualize praise as a management strategy. All parents praise, but they tend to do it reactively; in other words, if they happen to notice something, like an "A" on a test, they praise. Some parents heap on the praise with what seems like every other word. "That's great." "How wonderful." "I am so proud." In our experience, parents underestimate the power of praise. We encourage you to be proactive in your use of positive attention or praise. The reason for this is that children will engage in behaviors that increase a parent's attention to them. The best way to do this is to give your child specific behaviors to target as ways of getting positive attention from you. Target specific behaviors and look for opportunities to praise those behaviors. It is okay to focus on small behaviors such as speaking nicely to a sibling, or putting sneakers where they belong after taking them off. The key point is: *Make clear to your child the specific behaviors that you are praising.* General terms like "great" and "good," while encouraging, do not help children figure out just what it is you would like to see them do more often.

It is especially important to praise behaviors that are incompatible with behaviors you wish to decrease. For example, in one family we worked with, fighting among three siblings was driving their parents to despair. When they came for counseling, the parents said, "They are always fighting." Always? "Always. We get no peace." No peace? How horrible. Don't they sleep? "Of course they sleep." And have they been expelled from school? "No, they would never do those kinds of things at school. Only to each other." Do they ever fight as a pair? "In every way." Always? "Always." Where are they now? "They are in the waiting room." Oh. I can't hear them. Are they quiet when they fight? "They are as loud as can be." Well, they seem to not be fighting now, at least not much. "No, of course not…"

From this conversation we were able to identify some times when the kids did not fight. We advised the parents—*insisted* is probably the correct word—to look for instances of cooperation, or at least peaceful coexistence, and then praise the children for getting along with each other. We asked that they make their praise specific, and especially focus on when they truly felt their children were reasonably calm. It is important to praise specific behaviors ("You are sitting so nicely with your sister") rather than global qualities ("You are a good boy"), because specific praise serves to give children explicit information about what was praiseworthy, so they can repeat it. In addition, through praise, you are conveying what is important to you, what your values are. Praising a child for sharing teaches the child that kindness and generosity toward others is an important thing to do, will please you, and will make them feel good about themselves.

Often parents will ignore appropriate behavior, praise it half-heartedly, or use global praise because they are exhausted from attending to inappropriate behavior and do not expect praise to change anything. We warn them that if they do not follow through, they are unlikely to get success. Then we tell them that it's okay, we expect it will take at least a couple of weeks to get the hang of doing this.

SOME COMMON PRAISE TIPS

When praising, it is important to give unconditional rather than conditional praise. In other words, do not add the words "but" or "why" to the praise. Do not add "But what about this?" or "Why can't you do that all the time?" This type of qualification will negate the positive aspects of the praise.

Let's take four situations involving the fighting siblings we spoke of earlier. You see the following four things:

1. One of the kids helps another find a magazine without being asked to help him.
2. You have them all sitting at the dining room table to do their homework—and they actually are doing it.

3. After dinner, when they finish, they all get up and put their plates in the sink without being asked and without bumping and jostling each other.

4. Two kids who share a room clean it up after you ask them to, and have no problems with each other while doing it.

Think about how you might give some praise in each situation. Now take a look at some of our examples:

1. "I like the way you helped each other out."

2. "You did a great job sitting together and getting your homework done, without a single fight. Wow!"

3. "Thanks for taking your plates to the sink so carefully."

4. "You worked so well together, and your room looks great!"

See how easy it is to undo the praise by adding "but" and "why":

1. "I like the way you helped each other out. Why can't you always do this?"

2. "You did a great job sitting together and getting your homework done, without a single fight, but you really could have gotten even more done if you didn't talk so much."

3. "Thanks for taking your plates to the sink so carefully. Why don't you start doing it just that way every night?"

4. "You worked so well together, and your room looks great, but you didn't dust the dressers as well as I would like you to."

You can see clearly that adding these words changes the statements from praise to criticism or correctives. There is a time for each kind of statement. The point is to allow your praise to have the effect you want, and be satisfied with that—it's very powerful!

IGNORING IS HARDER THAN YOU THINK

Irritation is not just a skin condition. It is what many parents feel when their kids do all kinds of little, annoying, upsetting, disappointing things. When our skin is irritated, we often rub or scratch the area. It doesn't cure anything, and actually often makes matters worse. But it does bring a bit of temporary relief. When our kids irritate us, we "scratch" by issuing some statements about our annoyance, or maybe we just roll our eyes or shake our heads in a way that nonverbally tells our children we are not happy with them.

In response to kid irritation, try to ignore it. Mild, annoying, but harmless behaviors such as whining, interruptions, tantrums, and nagging should be things you work to ignore. Be warned, however, just as when you have an itch, ignoring kids' annoyances is extremely difficult to do. It is quite ironic that ignoring is more difficult than doing something. But ignoring actually involves a lot of work and EQ skills.

Before you start ignoring, prepare yourself for how much self-control it will take. You will have to be focused on your goal, learn to keep calm as you find yourself getting upset, and get ready for what is likely to happen next. When a behavior is ignored, the child will initially escalate the inappropriate behavior before he or she eventually stops. This has to do with normal learned behavior, and is not a plot by the child to try to drive you crazy. For example, when you turn the ignition key in a car, you expect it to start. If it does not start, you turn it again, and again, and a little longer, and harder, and start pushing the gas pedal. When you do something and expect something else to happen and it does not, you escalate the initial behavior. You think, "This worked before, so it should work again." Children think the same way. If you ignore a tantrum, the child knows this has gotten your attention before and assumes it will get your attention again. When you do not respond, the child does it more, and louder, and longer...until either he stops because he realizes it is not working, or he tries something else, like throwing something at you, that cannot be ignored because it is no longer harmless. (We'll talk about how to react to this kind of action, which we view as a violation of family rules, in the last section of this chapter.)

So, what does serious ignoring involve? It means no recognition of the child, and no eye contact. Also, no dirty looks, no reprimands, no rolling of eyes, muttering under one's breath, not even a heavy sigh—no attention at all. (Note that it is usually okay to inform children that they will be ignored.) Naturally, as soon as the child stops the inappropriate behavior, he should be praised for engaging in an appropriate behavior.

WHAT GETS YOUR GOAT?

To help build parents' emotional intelligence, we suggest that, as an exercise, you write down a list of things that bother you about your children. This can include such things as fighting among siblings, not listening, taking too long to get dressed, or complaining about homework. Prioritize the list from most important to least important. The bottom of the list (least important) will give you an idea of things to ignore. Now make a parallel list of opposite behaviors; for example, next to "fighting among siblings," you might write down "getting along with one another." This parallel list will give you an idea of things to praise. Start with the top of the list (most important) and target those items for praise.

FEEDBACK AND SELF-AWARENESS

We believe that children are basically good, know right from wrong, and want to do the right thing. What can get in their way is a lack of awareness of their feelings, impulse control, goals and plans, sensitivity towards others' feelings, and/or social skills— the basics of emotional intelligence. One way of helping children develop new skills is to monitor and give them feedback on their behavior. This works whether you are teaching math, golf, or the art of conversation. Keeping track of a behavior helps to increase the individual's self-awareness and ability to self-monitor. It can also help parents to view a particular behavior objectively and to see how bad it really is and whether it is getting any better or not.

PARENT (all right, it's probably a mom): You are getting crumbs all over the house.
CHILD: Sorry. (Or "I am not," or "It was my brother.")

What the child really wants to say, but either cannot or is smart enough to know not to, is, "Is that right? Well, let's look at this objectively. I have here a granola bar. Since it is a chewy thing, it is sticky and less likely to produce crumbs than, let's say, corn chips or pretzels. But crumbs can emerge. Now let's look at the area in which I walked with the offensive substance. I opened it in the kitchen. I took a bite. At that point, I was near the sink. I walked four steps into the dining room, whereupon another bite was consumed. Then I took an additional seven steps, while chewing, until I got to the back door. At that point, you issued your accusatory and inaccurate remark. Unless the size of our home has drastically decreased, and you have sublet the entire upstairs, living room, hallway, den, and stairway, as well as the basement and the porch and deck, crumbs did not get all over the house. In addition, the zone of maximum crumb dispersal would be where I took my bites, which can be carefully pinpointed. So I cannot really understand why you made that statement, unless you are not aware of the dimensions of your own home, or really thought I had wandered all over the house shaking my snack to create crumbs, or just wanted to unjustly accuse me and make things sound far worse than they really were. I am mystified. Would you like me to clean up all the spots that might have crumbs and next time try to keep the crumbs in the kitchen? *That* is something I can understand and go along with."

Keeping track of behaviors can be a bit of a pain in the neck.

It requires organization, consistency, and follow-through. If you monitor inconsistently, it gives the message to your child that you do not really care about the issue enough to do your (adult) part to address it, or that if the child is patient enough, parental will can be undermined in this area. However, monitoring behavior and giving feedback to a child are powerful tools that, as noted above, serve a variety of purposes and are well worth the effort.

Most behaviors can be monitored with the use of a chart. Setting up a chart is straightforward.

Goals. First, set some goals. What are the behaviors that you want to keep track of? Ideally, these should be phrased in a positive manner. We recommend that initially from one to three goals should be selected, depending on the parents' ability to consistently monitor the behavior. Other goals can always be added or cycled in once initial goals are met.

Goals may include sharing with siblings, using appropriate table manners, and completing homework independently. It is important to phrase goals positively, e.g., "Play nicely." We want to focus on increasing positive behaviors. There is, however, some merit in tracking a negative behavior. If you choose to do this, we suggest that you balance it with a positive behavior. For example, teasing or "put-downs" might be balanced by compliments, praise, or "put-ups." Hitting might be balanced by helping. Remember, at this stage of things, parents are not trying to change anything, but just to figure out what is happening, how often, when, and where.

Time frame. The time frame selected will depend on the goals. Usually the chart is set up with the days of the week across the top. Then, depending on the goal and your purposes, there may be a subdivision. For example, if homework is a goal, then under "Monday" there might be a choice of afternoon and evening, which really translate to after school and after dinner. On Saturday and Sunday, it might make more sense to just have A.M. and P.M., depending on your family's schedule. If table manners are the goal, "breakfast, lunch, snack, dinner" may be used for each day.

Scoring system. The scoring system again depends on the goals selected. Some goals lend themselves to counting the number of times they occur. In these cases, a mark can be put in the proper box in the chart each time the behavior takes place. When negative behavior is charted, it can be easier sometimes to take away a mark, rather than add one. For example, ten "happy faces" can be drawn in a goal/time square, and every time the child engages in the negative behavior (for example, when Todd hits his sister), one happy face is crossed out, or the happy face is turned into a sad face.

Charts are also extremely useful for monitoring behaviors outside of the home. For some children, report cards are not a useful form of feedback. The child does not make a connection between their behavior today in school and the grade they are going to get two months from now. Also, some children anticipate failure, so the only point in grades is to document what they see as their stupidity. Daily monitoring charts are time-consuming for teachers, but, again, for some children, they are well worth the effort. Having a child get feedback from the teacher throughout the day helps the child focus in on what is expected, ensures that the teacher will be giving both negative and positive feedback, and enables the parent to know what is going on. Most often when a parent asks, "How was school?" the answer is "Fine." The parent then asks, "What did you do today," and the child replies, "Nothing." The concerned and persistent parent asks, "Were there any problems?" to which the child answers in a bored manner, "No." By having a daily chart, the parent knows what kind of day it was. Then the parent can praise where appropriate and help the child problem-solve areas of deficiency.

THE INSIDE VIEW:
HOW CHARTING WORKS WITHOUT REWARDS

A mistake made by most parents who have done charts is to immediately introduce a reward for appropriate behavior. We disagree strongly. Motivation can be viewed as a target (see the accompanying figure). On the outside ring is material motivation—you do something because you get something in return. Social motivation, the middle ring, occurs we do something because it helps us to be with others or to gain approval from people we care about or want to impress. In the center is intrinsic motivation, which is doing something because of the satisfying feeling we get in doing it.

We are aiming for intrinsic motivation in children. If children are doing something for themselves, because it makes them feel good, and they are proud of their accomplishments, then nothing will stop them from doing it. They will do it because they want

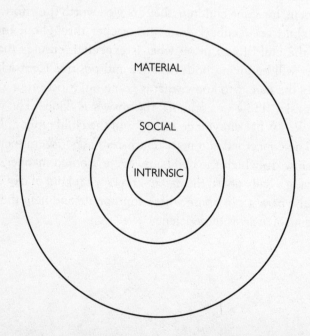

MATERIAL

SOCIAL

INTRINSIC

to do it. By giving children feedback on their performance, we are tapping into their intrinsic motivation to succeed.

Think of your children when they play a video game. What do they get? A score. This score alone motivates them, because they feel good about their accomplishment. How about the telephone? They don't even get a score for that. (You get a bill, but it comes a lot later than when the calls are made, which may be why you don't make as big a deal about the calls as you would if you got instant feedback about how much your kids' calls were costing you!)

It also is true that at least half of the time you monitor a behavior, you are going to change it. Why is that? Let's look at an example. If you want to lose weight, write down (honestly) everything you eat. Soon you will see that you are doing things you *know* you should not be doing. If you want to spend less money, write down everything you buy. Again, you will see spending that does not make sense.

Keeping track of behaviors makes us more conscious of them. Does this mean we are unconscious when we are doing them? Not exactly. We are on "automatic." We are doing something in the spirit of the moment, not thinking deeply about it, not reflecting on whether it is a good thing for us to do, whether it is consistent with our goals. When we have to write down items that we bought, and we know our spouses are going to review our list with us at some point and we will have to explain it, we are less inclined to spend frivolously.

Our kids are not especially inclined to "keep score" of what they are doing, but when they know there is a chart that will be reviewed by a parent, it gives them something else to think about. They become a bit more reflective—a hallmark of emotional intelligence—and less impulsive.

Social motivation tends to occur naturally in the environment, and also helps the child to develop intrinsic motivation. When children do well, they tend to receive positive feedback from others. This is generally how the world works: do nice things, and people will be nice to you.

Material motivation is farthest away from what we are aiming for. Children motivated in this way do things not because it makes them feel good or to please others, but because you are giving them something. When you no longer give them something, they will no longer do whatever it was that was being rewarded. If we want children to internalize good behavior, material reinforcement will not do it. It is interesting to note that in studies on why people leave their jobs, it is not money but lack of personal fulfillment or recognition from others that usually causes them to leave.

It is also interesting to note that if you give children an extrinsic motivator for something they are intrinsically motivated to do, you tend to deprive them of the intrinsic motivation. For example, if a child enjoys helping you in the kitchen (some children actually do) and you then pay the child to help, you may deprive the child of the intrinsic enjoyment of helping you. If you then stop paying the child, you are likely to diminish the child's motivation to help you.

On the other hand, there are times when material rewards can be valuable. For example, one child we worked with had experienced a great deal of academic failure because of a previously undiagnosed learning disability. This child would not do homework because he equated homework with frustration and failure. He did not associate homework with pride and achievement. No matter how much his homework was modified to be success-oriented, and no matter how much the parent praised homework-related behavior, it always turned into a battle. As a very insightful child said, "I'd rather be bad than stupid." In order for the child to work, the focus had to be taken off the child's self and placed on an external reward. In other words, the child would not work for himself or parental approval, but would work for a prize, because success or failure was not tied to his sense of self but to something external to himself. It was also necessary that the prize be worthwhile, i.e., something he really wanted. Once the child earned the prize, we could begin to get him to see that he really could do the work. This brought about a change in his self-perception from failure to someone who was competent. The seed of self-regard and intrinsic motivation was planted.

Another example of appropriate use of material reward occurs when you can be relatively sure that once the behavior is established, intrinsic motivation will take over. This is why rewards can be used for toilet training. Once the child is trained, they usually feel proud of themselves for being "big," and also receive lots of positive attention from others. This takes over for the material rewards, if they are used. Also, material rewards can be used to get hesitant children "over the hump." If a child is shy or inhibited, you can sometimes give him an incentive to participate in an activity, knowing that once he does it and adapts to it, he really will enjoy it. You can then safely withdraw the reward and he will continue to participate. When a material reinforcer is used, it should be carefully faded as soon as the child begins to experience success and positive feelings about himself. Remember, material reinforcement is a last resort, not an initial condition.

"Stuff Happens"

As we all know, in life, "stuff happens." That is just the way the world works. There are always consequences for our actions, some positive, some negative, some anticipated, some not. It is important for children to learn about the consequences of their actions. By applying the principle that "stuff happens," parents help children learn to anticipate and accept responsibility for their actions.

Whenever someone is given a command and a threat, such as, "You better do this or else I'm going to do that," it triggers what we call the "oppositional reflex." When we are intimidated or told what to do, our natural inclination is to say no. Children work the same way. When a parent threatens, "You'd better clean your room now, or you'll never go out again!" a child often reflexively begins to yell, argue, or refuse. You could overpower the child to get him to clean his room, but is this really the way you want to parent? (If you just answered "yes" to this rhetorical question, please reread chapter 1!)

When we say that "stuff happens," we are pointing out to our children, in a nonthreatening manner, the "stuff" that tends to happen as a result of their actions. Some of this may be clarified by doing the charting described earlier. We are all on the children's side, not against them. We are warning them about the things that might happen if they engage in a behavior, but they are free to do it anyway. For example, parents remind children that if they take a long time to complete their homework, or do it sloppily and have to redo it, they may miss television time.

The important aspect of "stuff happening" is that it is not the parent that teaches the child through a punishment; it is the consequence that teaches the child. This sidesteps power struggles and control issues. Remember, it is not a parent-versus-child situation. Parents are on the children's side, helping them to avoid aversive consequences in life. The parents' role is to warn the child about the consequence, not threaten it.

There is, of course, some controversy about this. We are not saying that whatever a child wants to do is okay. When there are issues of safety or matters of legality, efforts to stop a particular behavior are necessary. But this does not happen very often.

When explaining the potential consequence, parents should inform children in a matter-of-fact tone what will happen if they choose to engage in a certain behavior. The child should be given the choice of engaging in the behavior and experiencing the consequence or not. Even if the consequence is ultimately administered by the parent, the choice is the child's, and therefore the responsibility for experiencing the consequence is also the child's, not the parent's. What we know about emotional intelligence tells us that if the parent administers the warning and the consequence in anger, then the child will focus on the angry parent, rather than the consequence. When this happens, the lesson is lost.

When pointing out the stuff that happens, you can usually phrase it in an "If-then" form:

"If you finish your dinner, then you can have dessert."
"If you wear your coat, then you will be warm."
"If you take a long time getting ready for bed, then we won't have time for stories."
"If you do not drive safely, then you will not be able to use the car."

For some things, we cannot be quite as certain that the "stuff" will happen. So, we recommend you also use an "If-may" format:

"If you take the toy with you, you may lose it and be sad."
"If you don't study, you may not do well on the test."
"If you don't write a nice, prompt thank-you note, people may not be so generous with their gifts to you in the future."
"If you read the recipe, you may find that the food will be easier to cook and come out better."
"If you yell at your friends and don't share, they may not want to come over and play with you."

If the child chooses to engage in an inappropriate behavior and experience an aversive consequence, then the parent can be supportive rather than angry. "I'm sure you are upset about not watching your favorite TV show. I thought that might happen, and that's why I warned you about the time. How will you handle this next time? Maybe next time you'll be able to finish your homework before your show starts."

As noted earlier, parents cannot allow the child to engage in dangerous behaviors and potentially experience harmful consequences. "Honey, if you play in the busy street, then you may be hit by a car, and that would really hurt," is not an appropriate use of this technique. In this case, shouting, "Get out of the street now, there are cars coming!" is an appropriate use of the yelling technique we are all so familiar with. Also, saying, "If you put the knife in your mouth, then you will get blood all over the table," is also not recommended. In this case, we suggest taking away the knife until the child is old enough to use it properly. In these and other potentially harmful situations, you will need to take a more active role to ensure appropriate behavior.

Chill Out

Chill Out is our variation on "Time Out," which is a standard punishment that most parents have at least heard of, if not used. However, most parents use "Time Out" in a less-than-optimal manner. Partly this is because it is a lot harder to do correctly than it looks, and it only works when it is done correctly. We conceptualized Chill Out as a means of promoting self-direction within the family—both the parent's self-direction and the child's—rather than as a punishment.

Think of Chill Out as a substitute for yelling. The first step is to train yourself to say "Chill out," instead of yelling. This will help you stay in control with your children. If you think about it, parents tend to yell at children for two reasons: first, they do something they know they are not supposed to (this is a Rule Violation); second, they do not listen. Technically, this is Noncompliance with a Command. If it is a Rule Violation, the consequence is immediate. No discussion, no debate, no warning, no negotiation, just Chill Out. If it is Noncompliance with a Command, you are allowed a command, then repeat the command once, then Chill Out. Remember to avoid repeating rules or commands because each time you restate the rule or command, you may get a little angrier. Eventually, you end up out of control yourself. It's not cool to scream "Chill out" to your kids!

The procedure outlined below teaches self-direction because, for children aged five and up, the child, not you, puts himself or herself in Chill Out. Emotionally Intelligent Parenting involves knowing that you cannot calm your children; they must do it themselves. Obviously we can do things that give them more of a chance to get under better control. Initially, what they need is time to learn to calm down and an incentive to do it. Chill Out affords them both.

HOW TIME OUT AND CHILL OUT REALLY WORK

It is common among parents to think of Time Out and Chill Out as punishments. But they are not. Instead, they are teaching tools. The basic idea is captured here in a script we help parents to use with their children.

Dear Child of Mine,
Being with other people is a privilege. You get to play with others, watch TV with them, talk with them, use others' games and toys. To be with other people, you must behave with a certain amount of respect and follow some basic rules. If you cannot behave in a socially reasonable manner, in a way that does not hurt or upset others, then you will not have the privilege of being with others, and you will not be able to do all the things that happen when you are with others. To help you learn to get along with others, you will have a chance to Chill Out. You can think about what you have done, away from others. After you have had a chance to Chill Out, then you will get to go back with others. Hopefully, you will get along and stay with others. But if the same kinds of things happen again, we figure it is just your way of telling us that you need more Chilling Out. And you can Chill Out as long and as often as you need to, until you have the self-control to stay with others and concentrate on having fun. Then you will not need to Chill Out much, if at all. Oh, by the way, if you try to run out of Chill Out, or if you don't do it when I tell you, that is your way of saying that you really have a lot of self-control to learn. That's okay! In that case, I will carry you or hold you until you are able to

sit and Chill Out by yourself. I will be your self-control until you have enough on your own.

Chill Out is appropriate for children between the ages of two and twelve. Chill Out decreases a problem behavior by dramatically withdrawing attention from the child when he engages in that behavior. It is important that the words "Chill Out" are sacred. When you say them, you have to really mean them. Once you say them, nothing else can happen until the child goes to Chill Out.

Initially, you need to make the sacrifices necessary to implement Chill Out correctly. So either be willing to be late for work or do not say "Chill Out"; instead, use another technique. Once you have made the investment in teaching Chill Out and having the child learn to calm himself, accept your authority, and sit quietly, it can be a very effective tool that ends up taking less time than nagging, yelling, and arguing. When doing Chill Out, remember that you are doing it so that you stay in control and so that your child learns self-direction.

Chill Out should be done with a minimum of talking. You do not remind the child of the rule prior to Chill Out, and you do not repeat the command over and over. Also, when sending the child to Chill Out, you are allowed to say ten words or less. It is important not to have a conversation with your child because Chill Out works by withdrawing attention and talking is attention. Also, when a child has done something wrong and is going to be disciplined, he or she is not listening to you anyway, so save your breath and spare yourself aggravation. If your child wants to know why he is being sent to Chill Out, explain it afterwards. If he wants to explain to you why he was justified in hitting his sister, have him mount his defense after he Chills Out. For those of you who are thinking, "Yeah, great, but my kid won't go and won't stay," read on. We have that—and many other possibilities—covered.

THE CHILL OUT PROCEDURE

1. Explain to the child the behaviors you expect him to engage in and those behaviors you expect him to refrain from. Tell the child about Chill Out and when you will be using it.

2. Establish a Chill Out spot. It should be safe and boring. It should also be easily accessible, and you should be able to monitor the child while in Chill Out. A chair in a little-used room, or a step on a staircase, is usually a good place. Do not use the bathroom, the TV room, the kitchen, or the child's bedroom.

3. Use Chill Out for rule violations and noncompliance. Place the child in Chill Out immediately when he violates a house rule. If the child does not comply with a command, repeat the command once with a warning, then place her in Chill Out if she does not comply.

4. When the child has violated a rule or not complied with a command, using ten words or less, tell the child to sit in Chill Out. Try to stay calm and matter-of-fact. Set a timer for two to ten minutes, depending on the age of the child. When the timer rings, the child can come out of Chill Out. If the child makes significant noise in Chill Out or comes out before the time is up, restart the timer from the beginning. Do not let the child go to the bathroom during Chill Out. (Don't fall for this one; he can hold it.)

5. If a preschool child resists going to Chill Out, it may be necessary to restrain him gently until the time is up. If a school-age child resists going to Chill Out, add one minute for each refusal, up to five additional minutes. If the child still does not go to Chill Out, remove up to three privileges, one at a time (e.g., television, going outside, dessert). If the child persists in his refusal to go to Chill Out, place him in his room until he is ready to go to Chill Out (the time in the room does not count as Chill Out). Be careful not to give the child additional attention for his refusal to cooperate with Chill Out. Be as brief as possible with the above procedure. Any discussion or explanation should occur *after* the Chill Out.

6. After Chill Out, allow the child to return to the situation he was in. If he engages in an appropriate behavior, praise him; if he engages in another inappropriate behavior, repeat Chill Out.

7. Always attend to and positively reinforce appropriate behaviors, especially those incompatible with the problem behavior. As soon as possible after Chill Out, look for an appropriate behavior to reinforce.

A FINAL WORD

Certain things happen in households in which Emotionally Intelligent Parenting is practiced. They are households in which praise can be heard regularly; there is a sense of goals and priorities to guide family actions; few threats are used; and there is a tendency to let children learn from their experiences. But this does not mean everything is acceptable. When behavior gets out of control and children need to increase their self-discipline, they are given a chance to Chill Out and think about what they have done before they get back to doing what they were doing "pre-Chill." Finally, parents realize that when there are certain behaviors they want to encourage or discourage, they can focus their children's attention on it by charting it. From feedback comes greater reflection and self-awareness, which then leads to increased self-discipline and better self-management.

Will these ideas be all you see parents doing? Not likely. But as households get a better balance between the usual parental discipline methods and the ones we have presented, children will be more likely to develop *Self*-direction and *Self*-discipline—the goal of all parents.

Chapter 5

How Children Can Be Less Impulsive and Build Self-Control and Social Skills

■   ■   ■

DAVE: (offering a cigarette): Want one?
MARK: Nah.
DAVE: Why not?
Mark shrugs.
DAVE: Wimp.
MARK: Shut up.
DAVE: Don't you smoke?
Mark shrugs again.
DAVE: Just try it, it's no big deal.
Mark looks uncomfortable.
DAVE: C'mon. (Hands him a cigarette and lights it.)
Mark coughs.
DAVE: Wimp. (Laughs.)
Mark continues to smoke.

Is there a parent who does not dread his or her child being either Dave or Mark? How will children learn to deal effectively with their strong feelings, use self-control in stressful situations, and communicate assertively with others? Is this really important, you might ask. Yes—research indicates these skills are critical to success in school, in one's family, with friends, and on the job.

If our children are not aware of their feelings, they will find it difficult to control impulsive actions and decision-making; they also will not be able to communicate clearly what they really mean. For example, in the vignette above, if a child's friends are smoking cigarettes, he may have several conflicting feelings. He may feel insecure and want to be a part of the group, he may be fearful of getting into trouble if he smokes, and he may be excited about doing something "grown-up." Parents may hope their children will focus on the fear, but chances are that early adolescents will focus mostly on their feelings of insecurity. If children are taught to be aware of these feelings, it may lead them to realize that doing something harmful to themselves is not the smartest way to deal with insecurity—nor will it create a lot of future security.

Self-control also is strongly involved in situations like this. Children need to be able to handle constructively their insecurity, fear, and excitement. Joining in such activities as smoking may be one way of coping with their feelings, but we want children to know other coping techniques for dealing with intense feelings. In addition, children need to know how to say no in an assertive manner. Finally, we want children to be able to approach these situations armed with critical thinking skills so that they can make good decisions for themselves rather than be swayed by the crowd.

The emotional regulation, self-control, and social skills introduced in this chapter are prerequisites to the thinking skills that will be introduced in the next chapter. If children learn to sort out their feelings, to react to stress in ways that are not impulsive, and to communicate effectively with others, then they will have a better chance to respond to social situations in a thoughtful and responsible manner. These are skills that can be taught and learned like any others. The following activities will help you build your children's skills in these important areas.

Emotional Intelligence Principles Highlighted in This Chapter's Activities

☞ 1. Be Aware of One's Own Feelings and Those of Others
   2. Show Empathy and Understand Others' Points of View
☞ 3. Regulate and Cope Positively with Emotional and Behavioral Impulses
   4. Be Positive Goal- and Plan-Oriented
☞ 5. Use Positive Social Skills in Handling Relationships

AWARENESS OF FEELINGS

Our feelings are the signals that let us know when we have problems. It is clearly important for children to learn to be aware of their feelings, but this is often difficult for adults to do, let alone children. Some children seem to have transmission problems: they don't have different gears and speeds. They are either on or off, but lack the range of reactions in between. For example, some children are either "good" or "mad." When someone bothers them, they quickly go from "good" to "mad" without awareness of the range of emotions along the way, such as annoyed, inconvenienced, irritated, upset, hurt, angry, and furious.

What kids need is a broader "feelings vocabulary." With just a few changes in your routines, you can help your children shift their gears much more effectively as they face various situations at home, at school, and with their friends. It is not hard to do; when the family sits around the dinner table and discusses politics, the children will learn politics. If the family talks about feelings, the children will learn to identify and express feelings. When a parent asks children about their day, it is important to ask also how children *felt* about what happened.

Throughout the day, parents' conversations with their children can include asking them how something made them feel and how other people involved might have felt. It is also important for parents to talk about their feelings when talking about *their* day—an example of modeling. Through such small measures, carried out occasionally as opportunities present themselves, parents are making large contributions toward increasing their children's awareness of feelings, ability to express them, and the development of empathy for others' feelings. If one listens closely to conversations, even intimate family conversations, it is surprising how rarely feelings are discussed. But feelings may be the most important aspect of whatever the person is saying, especially from an emotional intelligence point of view.

FEELINGS CHARADES

Feelings Charades is a family game that can be played to increase awareness of feelings. In this game, a variety of feeling words can be written down (or you can use pictures of facial expressions of feelings cut out from magazines, especially for younger children) and placed in a hat or paper bag. The first person picks a feeling from the hat and acts it out without speaking while other family members guess what the feeling was. This helps both the actor and the audience to identify words, facial characteristics, and other nonverbal cues of feelings.

A similar activity is called "Feelings Flashback." For this game, the same cards with feelings words or pictures are used. A person picks one and shares a time when they experienced that particular feeling. To make it more specific, the following questions can be asked:

Who was with you?
What were you doing?
When was this?
Where were you?

How did you know you felt this way?

Why do you think you felt that way?

Each family member can then talk about a time when they, too, felt this way. This teaches three things. First, family members share feelings in an atmosphere of assurance that it is okay to have these feelings because they are normal. Second, parents can model their own reactions so children can better learn how to identify their own feelings. And, third, it can help everyone develop greater empathy for others, and it furthers communication among family members.

For example, Maggie, age nine, picked the feeling card titled Scared, and said in response to the above questions:

Who: "I was alone."

What: "I was trying to go to sleep."

When: "At night."

Where: "In my bed."

How: "I had a headache and my stomach hurt and I was crying."

Why: "I don't know, I was just scared. I didn't want to be alone."

Dad then shared a time when he got scared at night lying in bed. Mom shared a similar situation, and Maggie's younger sister talked about monsters, at which everyone got a good laugh.

FEELINGS ON TV

Another important activity in teaching identification of feelings is to watch television with your children. Television encourages passive acceptance of the values (or lack of values) being imparted by the show. We believe in teaching children to become active viewers and to look critically at what they are watching.

For example, even on "family" shows, people talk to each other in rude and hurtful ways while the television audience response encourages viewers at home to laugh. This teaches children that it is good to laugh at others' pain. If you watch with your child and ask, "Gee, when one brother called the other brother an idiot, how do you think it made him feel?" you are teaching many positive skills. You are helping your children learn emotional identification, anticipation of emotional consequences in others, empathy, and independent thinking. You can follow up this question with something like, "Well, if that made him feel bad, why did everyone laugh?" This will get your child to think critically rather than just to laugh along with the crowd at others' misfortune. (A possible additional benefit if you watch television with your children in this manner is that it may diminish their enjoyment of it and their motivation to continue watching. They may then actually turn it off to exercise some real-life social skills, perhaps by playing with others!)

PICTURES ARE WORTH A THOUSAND WORDS

Art projects with children are another way to encourage "feelings vocabulary" development. You can cut out pictures from a magazine for a "feelings collage," or draw a picture depicting a feeling such as "excitement." Use of the computer, either through a drawing program or a storytelling program, is another way of engaging children in a motivating activity to promote emotional intelligence.

STOREFRONTS

Another enjoyable activity for families is "Storefronts." We could have also called it "Sidewalk Café" because it comes from the age-old recreation of people-watching. Because malls seem to have become the modern American sidewalk, we call it "Storefronts" instead. To get this activity started, you point out the front window of a store in a mall or other shopping area, and ask what the window tells about the store. Encourage a careful look at all aspects of the window—what is there, what might have been there, why things are placed where they are, the colors used, and so on. Then you say to your children that a person's public exterior also reveals something about him. Pick a couple of people to observe, and have your children guess something about them. Look at their facial expressions, how they carry themselves, their voices if you can hear them, their clothing. Can you guess their feelings? Where they are going? How long have they been shopping? It is especially instructive to observe parent-child interactions. What seems to be going on between them? How does the child look and/or sound? How much does this look like us?

COLOR CONNECTION

This variation on the time-honored psychological technique of word association is a way of building a feelings vocabulary. This is a good game to play in a car or while waiting in line. Start with a physical characteristic and associate a color with it. For example, one person says "tall," and the other person has to say what color it makes them think of. Other prompting words can be *hot, cold, fat, big, tiny, curvy.* Prompting words can often come just from looking around wherever you are. After this, give your child a feeling word (*happy, angry, excited, sad*) and ask what colors come to mind. You can use any category of words to get things started, such as shapes, trees, flowers, or TV characters. Another way of doing this is to point out something in the environment and ask what feeling is associated with it. For example, in the car, you might pass an old house or a large tree and ask what feeling it elicits in family members.

KEEP CALM

Were you ever in an argument with someone and they told you to calm down? Wasn't that helpful? Didn't you respond by thanking them for making you aware that you were getting out of control? No? We are not surprised. Believe it or not, children do not appreciate being told to calm down, either. The reason for this is that *you* cannot calm others down; they can only calm themselves down. For example:

JENNY (age fourteen, on coming home from her father's house): I hate him, I'm not going there again.

MOM: What did he do to you?

JENNY: You always think he did something. Why do you accuse him all the time! I hate it when you do that!

MOM: Would you calm down? I didn't say anything. What happened. Tell me!

JENNY (storming off): "No. Nothing. Leave me alone."

In this scenario, the mother is understandably upset. However, instead of opening a dialogue with her daughter, the mother enlarges the conflict and it becomes between mother and daughter as well as between father and daughter and, likely, between mother and father.

Another example:

TOM (age nine): Sue is such an idiot. She's so mean.

MOM: Honey, what's the matter?

TOM (sobbing): She's the matter.

MOM: Okay, I understand you are really upset by something that happened with your sister. Before we talk about it, let's both take a deep breath...come on, do it with me...that's good, now slowly out your mouth...how are you doing? Let's do it again...Okay, can you tell me what happened?

TOM (calmer and more in control): I hate her.

MOM: I know you are really upset right now. Are you ready to talk about it?

TOM: Okay.

In this case the mother realized that Tom was upset and not yet able to discuss the problem in a productive manner. Therefore, it was necessary to first help him regain a degree of composure. Rather than just telling Tom to calm down so they could talk about it, the mother walked the child through a calming exercise. The mother's use of the breathing technique probably also helped her to stay calm in this situation.

THE KEEP CALM ACTIVITY

If being aware of feelings is the first step, controlling upsetting feelings is the next. The Keep Calm activity is designed to help children and parents stop and think prior to acting. It is a means of reducing impulsive behavior and separating emotional reaction from cognitive and behavioral reaction. This can then foster action based on thoughtfulness, in addition to whatever is affecting the child. The objectives of Keep Calm are to:

1. Point out problematic situations where self-control can be used to calm down before reacting.
2. Teach, through a deep-breathing and stress-distracting exercise, how to get calm and keep self-control in a problematic situation.
3. Practice a deep-breathing and stress-distracting exercise.

Here is the Keep Calm activity:

Keep Calm is something that will help you get ready to solve problems and handle times when you feel hassled and upset. There are four simple steps to remember:

1. Tell yourself, "Stop and take a look around."
2. Tell yourself, "Keep calm."
3. Take a deep breath through your nose while you count to five, hold it while you count to two, then breathe out through your mouth while you count to five.
4. Repeat these steps until you feel calm.

M. Elias and J. Clabby, *Social Decision Making Skills:*
A Curriculm Guide for the Elementary Grades, New Brunswick, N.J.:
Center for Applied Psychology, Rutgers University, 1989.

Keep Calm should be taught, practiced, and reinforced before the need has clearly arisen. If families have practiced this exercise in less stressful situations, they are more likely to use the skill when they really need to.

HOW DO I START?

The best time to start is when a situation comes up like the one between Tom and his mom. Then it is in the child's interest to calm down so that he or she can get out the story. Afterwards, that situation can be used as a reminder: "Remember when you were upset and we did a little breathing so that you could calm down and tell me what happened? That's something that I find helpful to do at other times when I feel stressed or upset." Parents can then give a couple of examples, ideally of things that the child might have seen, such as when the newspaper was delivered into the flowerbed or when dinner was interrupted for the third time in ten minutes by a courtesy call, or when there was a lot of deadline pressure at work. At this point you may want to share with your children *how* you know when you are stressed.

FEELINGS FINGERPRINTS

Children need to understand that our bodies send us signals that we are about to lose our self-control. These signals are signs of feeling upset or stressed, and we call them "Feelings Fingerprints." Like fingerprints, everybody has them; but also like fingerprints, everyone's are unique. Some people get headaches, a nervous stomach, a stiff neck, or sweaty palms. Some get all four. Others get a dry mouth, a quick heartbeat, clenched fists, flushed face, or itchy skin. When parents find themselves in a stressful or difficult choice situation, they can verbalize how they are feeling and what their Feelings Fingerprints are. This segues naturally into asking kids, "You just heard how my body sends me a headache behind my left eye and a stomachache when I am upset and under stress. How do *your* bodies let *you* know when you are upset?"

Children then take their turn generating examples of situations during which they felt upset, and what their Feelings Fingerprints were. We call those events "Trigger Situations." Feelings Fingerprints are helpful because they warn us that we are in a tough situation and need to use our self-control to keep calm. Parents may want to use this opportunity to discuss with children what it means to use self-control. Ask them to tell you of different times and situations in which they have to use self-control. *Then ask for ways in which they show self-control, or things they do to keep self-control.*

After this, continue by making the point that, at one time or another, everyone finds himself in a conflict that needs to be resolved. These can be problems in school or with peers, with a teacher, parents, or friends. "Sometimes we might jump right into trying to deal with a problem before we are ready. The breathing that you did is really something called 'Keep Calm,' and it helps people—both children and parents—to learn how to stay calm and keep self-control during a conflict. This way we can be ready to deal with the problem by thinking before we act." Finally, make the point that when someone bothers them, when they are in a tough situation, when they are in some other Trigger Situation, or when they notice their Feelings Fingerprints, *it is important to Keep Calm before trying to solve the problem.* (Keep Calm should also be used by parents themselves prior to calling for a Chill Out or trying to ignore a child.)

With this introduction, the Keep Calm steps can be introduced and practiced. As a family activity, a Keep Calm poster or two can be made and put up in a prominent place in the house, such as the kitchen or television room. The poster can serve as a reminder to use this skill.

Keep Calm works to produce self-control in four stages:

1. Repetition of the Keep Calm steps out loud, with the parent prompting use of each step individually.

2. Repetition of the Keep Calm steps to oneself in a whisper and using the entire procedure when prompted.

3. Silent and spontaneous repetition of Keep Calm by the child (and parent).

4. Reminders to use Keep Calm when Trigger Situations come up or are anticipated.

Here are examples of how to practice all four stages:

1. Have the family read the Keep Calm steps out loud. Then have the family engage in a physical activity (such as jumping jacks or running in place). After one or two minutes of activity, say, "All right, let's use Keep Calm. Say 'stop'...say 'keep calm'... take a deep breath through your nose while counting to five, hold it to a count of two, breathe out through your mouth to a count of five. Are you starting to feel calm?" (As necessary, repeat Keep Calm.)

2. Use a similar physical activity, except start the children by saying, "When I say 'Now,' use Keep Calm to calm yourselves down. Say the Keep Calm in a whisper. Look at the poster if you forget the steps."

3. At the third stage, when the children are getting a little wild, ask them to use Keep Calm silently. Develop signals or cues for the children to use to tell you when they are calm.

4. It is important for adults to continue to prompt the use of Keep Calm when a child is upset or beginning to lose control; it can also be used prior to tests, school plays, or any other anxiety-provoking or Trigger Situation. (For older children, situations such as school dances, job interviews, and peer pressure to try dangerous or antisocial actions are times to use Keep Calm.) Bedtimes and family meetings are good times to review children and parents' use of Keep Calm and how they might have done an even better job. The more children are prompted to use Keep Calm and other social problem-solving strategies, the more quickly they will master them.

In addition to a poster or sign with the Keep Calm steps, Keep Calm can be reinforced through several activities. Have children keep a list of situations that are coming up or in which they can anticipate using Keep Calm will be helpful to them. Also have them keep track of when Keep Calm should have been used. Present children with difficult situations, and practice preparing for those difficult and upsetting situations by using Keep Calm.

Some children, especially older ones, may balk at using Keep Calm. It can be helpful to introduce it as an exercise developed by sports psychologists and trainers of musicians of all kinds to enhance athletic and musical performance (which it is). Discuss with them anxiety provoking situations (asking someone for a date, going for a job interview) and how anxiety interferes in performance. Ask them to watch athletes (baseball batters, basketball players taking a foul shot, and Olympic divers give especially good demonstrations) prior to performing a feat that requires concentration and skill in the face of stress. Point out to the children that the athletes take a breath or engage in a self-calming activity. This is exactly what Keep Calm is. Then encourage them to apply these points to their own social and academic "performances." If you can, get your child's sports coach to teach Keep Calm to the whole team.

Keep Calm will also be more powerful if parents model its use, make lists of Trigger Situations, and in other ways *show that self-control is not for children only.* Here is an example of the use of Keep Calm with one of the authors' children.

KEEP CALM IN ACTION: A FATHER-DAUGHTER EXAMPLE

My (BSF) daughter is actively involved in a theater workshop group with other children between the ages of five and seventeen. Over a four-month period, the children put on several full-length musical productions that are performed for parents, schools, and community groups. My daughter has learned to handle her emotions and work effectively in this multi-age theater group. She quickly learned the full range of emotions as she began the fall season. It is always nerve-racking for my daughter to prepare a small audition piece when she returns to perform each semester. Using Keep Calm certainly helps allay her anxiety as she approaches the stage to audition in front of the director and the other students in the program. With a sense of calm, my daughter approaches the stage and is able to focus on the task that is set out before her, knowing that this short audition can make or break her season and determine the parts she will receive.

But this is only the start! Working effectively with the children is another task that must be mastered when working in a theater workshop group. As the competition to receive starring roles rises, so do jealousy and competitiveness among the children. As each member of the group vies for leading roles, the children must learn to deal with rather strong emotional feelings. Though my daughter has been fortunate to receive leading roles, it has often presented her with the problem of how the other children in the group react to her.

During the past season, one of my daughter's friends told my daughter, "I hate you, I wanted the leading part in *Oklahoma.*" It would have been easy for my daughter to get defensive and hostile toward her friend, but she was able to avoid doing this, which defused the situation. Such interactions as this happen throughout the course of the season, and the ways in which they are resolved—or not—determine the effectiveness of the children working together.

BE YOUR BEST FOR CONFIDENT COMMUNICATION

As noted previously, social and emotional intelligence is a complex thing. No one technique, skill, or approach is going to "solve" every problem or teach thoughtful decision-making. Emotional intelligence is developed in interconnected layers, a bit like vanilla ice cream with fudge swirl. Here is another flavor to add to the mix:

In addition to awareness of feelings and some degree of self-control over intense feelings, it is necessary for children to assert themselves through *confident communication*. Children need to distinguish between passive, aggressive, and confident styles of behavior.

Confident communication can be summarized as being one's BEST. In order to be one's BEST, awareness of four key components are necessary:

B   **Body posture** (Stand up straight, be confident in yourself, but not arrogant.)

E   **Eye contact** (Look at the person appropriately; cultures differ on this dimension.)

S   **Speech** (Use appropriate language, say what you really feel, but don't be insulting; no put-downs.)

T   **Tone of voice** (Use a calm voice, no whispering or shouting.)

BEST is a way of communicating with others that enables someone to be sure of himself and increase the chance of being understood and respected by others.

Parents can explain that there are three different ways in which one person can communicate with another. People who use these methods can be called the Blaster (aggressive), the Shrinker (passive), or the Me (confident).

The Blaster is aggressive, pushy, and bossy toward others. The Blaster does not care about other people's feelings and tries to get what she wants by bullying others. She knows what she wants and tries to get it, but does not take into consideration other factors and people in trying to get what she wants. The parent can help children anticipate what might happen if the Blaster tries to get what she wants in an aggressive way. Although she may sometimes get what she wants, others will not like her, and this may interfere with her ability to get what she wants in the long run. There are many examples of this at home. Ask the child, "If you yell at me, do I do what you want?" (We hope you don't.)

The Shrinker is meek and passive. The Shrinker seems to care more about what others want than what he wants. The Shrinker does not stand up for himself or really try to get what he wants. The Shrinker lets others walk all over him. Although the Shrinker avoids conflict, he never really gets what he wants.

Obviously, the Me takes a more positive approach than the Blaster and the Shrinker. The Me knows what she wants and is not afraid to ask for it. However, she also takes into consideration other people's feelings and rights. The Me says what she feels, but in a way that others can listen to her. The Me knows she can't have what she wants all the time, but also knows that the best way to try is to work with others.

BEST is a way of helping children act more like a Me than a Blaster or a Shrinker. Older children find the BEST skills relevant, but are less likely to relate to the Blaster, the Shrinker, and the Me. However, they can generate examples of "too much" and "too little" BEST behavior and then create their own labels. Many children also find that they can label the Blaster and Shrinker with the names of people they know, or television or movie characters. Sometimes a positive model can be used as a reminder of the "Me." It is often useful to raise BEST in the context of a common problem, such as talking to friends, dating, entering a group, job and other interviews, or starting new situations like camp or after-school clubs or sports.

Here are two additional BEST activities for use at different times.

HOLLYWOOD'S BEST

To help make sure our children draw positive messages from movies and videos they watch, we can ask them how characters expressed certain feelings. Using BEST as a guideline, we can ask them about their body language, eye contact, the speech they use, and their tone of voice. We can model our impressions of important points in a movie and ask other family members if they saw things the same way. It is especially useful, when characters handle things violently, to ask how they could have used BEST to be successful without being a Blaster.

FAMILY BEST

Relatives are coming over. Or maybe you are visiting others. That tough moment is almost at hand—greeting everyone without offending anyone. Not to worry—this time it will work out the BEST ever. Just use BEST to rehearse your family. When Grandpa Jaime comes in, stand straight but not too straight; don't look him right in the eyes, keep your eyes down, call him "sir," and make sure your tone of voice is quiet but not too soft. And when Sheila brings in the new baby, there are other BEST rules to follow. You get the idea—when contacts are going to be made with families and others, job interviews, public speaking, and the like, BEST can be part of your family members' preparation.

TROUBLE TRACKERS

Trouble Trackers are a way of beginning to put skills together to reduce family conflict and improve children's independent problem-solving. A Trouble Tracker is a worksheet that can be completed by children to encourage them to think about a problem and how to solve it before discussing it with a parent. For example, two siblings are fighting. Both siblings get sent to Chill Out. After Chilling Out, they are encouraged to use Keep Calm. Then each is given a Trouble Tracker to complete. After that, the parent discusses the Trouble Trackers with both children, who are prompted to use their BEST behaviors.

There are two versions of Trouble Trackers, depending on the reading and writing levels of the child (see samples that follow). For younger children, a picture of the problem and other parts of the Tracker can be drawn. For some kids, it will be necessary to help them write out their answers. You may want to try having them tape-record their answers, or use the computer (something we will say more about in chapter 7).

USES OF TROUBLE TRACKERS

1. Annoyed by persistent whining? Ask your child to complete a Trouble Tracker—preferably in silence. Do this consistently, and you will find that it will cut down on the whining and encourage your child to think of another way of reacting to problems or frustrations or disappointment.

2. In one family, the children arrived home several hours before the parents and invariably got into a fight and called the mother at work. Fortunately, there was a fax machine at home. The children were instructed to complete a Trouble Tracker and fax it to the parent before calling. This cut down on calls, prompted the children to begin thinking about solving the problem before calling, and gave the parent a sense of the problem before the phone call.

3. When children are faced with a stressful situation outside the family, they can also complete a Trouble Tracker and then discuss it with a parent.

A SAMPLE TROUBLE TRACKER

The following Trouble Tracker was completed by one sibling who was being annoyed by another. The Trouble Tracker had been discussed with both children as a vehicle to help them resolve conflicts between them. Whenever there was a conflict, they were to complete a Trouble Tracker as a first step. Or, if they wanted to complain about one another, they first had to complete a Trouble Tracker and give it to their mother (this was a single-parent household).

TROUBLE TRACKER

Name: Jim   Date: Monday

WHERE WERE YOU?
In my house.

WHAT HAPPENED?
She made fun of me, and I got angry so I kicked her.

WHO ELSE WAS INVOLVED?
Nobody.

WHAT DID YOU DO?
I kicked her.

WHAT DID THE OTHER PEOPLE DO?
Made fun of me.

HOW DID YOU FEEL? HOW DID THE OTHER PEOPLE FEEL?
Angry.

HOW DO YOU THINK YOU HANDLED YOURSELF?

1	2	3	4	5
poorly	not so well	okay	good	(great)

HOW UPSET WERE YOU?

1	2	3	4	5
(mad)	really upset	pretty upset but okay	a little upset	not upset at all

WHAT ARE SOME OTHER THINGS YOU COULD HAVE DONE?
Tell my mom, kick her harder, give her a dead arm.

WHAT ARE SOME THINGS YOU CAN DO NOW TO EITHER
FIX THE PROBLEM OR PREVENT IT IN THE FUTURE?
Nothing.

The preceding example was a very useful Trouble Tracker, for two reasons. First, completing it did help stop the immediate conflict. Rather than the mother trying to sort out who did what to whom, and why, this gave her at least some parts of the story. Second, because it took several minutes to write, the child was calmer afterwards and more receptive to talking about the problem. This particular Trouble Tracker also tells us a lot about where this child is in his level of emotional intelligence. He is aware of his feelings and able to verbalize the problem and what he did to try to solve it. However, he lacks the ability to self-evaluate accurately; for instance, he indicated that he handled himself "great," which one might disagree with. He also has difficulty generating effective problem-solving solutions. His "tell my mom" solution is likely just there for show, and his more realistic aggressive solutions will not solve the problem, but only make it worse. He is going to need some assistance in learning how to create solutions. However, his last response is perhaps the most revealing. When asked what he can do now, he responded, "Nothing." This answer indicates his feelings of futility and hopelessness. He believes that there is nothing he can do to fix or prevent the problem, so why should he really try? This suggests that the child does not need punishment, which will only further demoralize him, but parental support and encouragement.

Having your child fill out a Trouble Tracker will allow you to read him better, and then enable you to take the steps needed to help build the skills he needs.

TROUBLE TRACKER

Name:_____Date:_____

WHERE DID THE PROBLEM HAPPEN?

on the bus	in the hall	on the playground
at home	in the yard	at a friend's house
at school	at lunch	in my room

Other:_____

WHAT HAPPENED?

someone bothered me	someone hurt me	someone cursed at me
someone teased me	someone kicked me	someone called me a name
someone hit me	I got frustrated	
	I lost it	

Other:_____

WHO WAS IT? _____

I FELT:

bad	upset	embarrassed	scared	mean
sad	worried	angry	annoyed	ticked
mad	steamed	hurt	bothered	happy

Other:_____

THEN I:

hit them	bothered them	didn't play with them
hurt them	told an adult	ran away
ignored them	made a face	talked to them as
called them a name	used Keep Calm	my BEST
	walked away	

WHAT I LIKED ABOUT WHAT I DID:

WHAT I DID NOT LIKE ABOUT WHAT I DID:

WHAT I WOULD DO NEXT TIME:

TROUBLE TRACKER

WHERE WERE YOU?

WHAT HAPPENED?

WHO ELSE WAS INVOLVED?

WHAT DID YOU DO?

WHAT DID THE OTHER PEOPLE DO?

HOW DID YOU FEEL? HOW DID THE OTHER PEOPLE FEEL?

HOW DO YOU THINK YOU HANDLED YOURSELF?

1	2	3	4	5
poorly	not so well	okay	good	great

HOW UPSET WERE YOU?

1	2	3	4	5
mad	really upset	pretty upset but okay	a little upset	not upset at all

WHAT ARE SOME OTHER THINGS YOU COULD HAVE DONE?

WHAT ARE SOME THINGS YOU CAN DO NOW TO EITHER FIX THE PROBLEM OR PREVENT IT IN THE FUTURE?

A Final Word

In this chapter we have presented some of the most powerful and practical tools of Emotionally Intelligent Parenting: Feelings Fingerprints, Keep Calm, Be Your BEST, and Trouble Trackers. They allow parents to help children identify their feelings and improve their self-control. The Trouble Trackers have been used tens of thousands of times by parents and children to keep track of their attempts at self-discipline and improve them. The next step is to add a strategy for problem-solving and decision-making that can be used in a variety of everyday situations, both simple and complicated. That is the focus of chapter 6.

Chapter 6

Coaching Your Children in Responsible Action: FIG TESPN to the Rescue

■ ■ ■

FIG TESPN? (pronounced Fig TES-pin). Who is FIG TESPN? Who is FIG TESPN for? Why is FIG TESPN important? How can you bring FIG TESPN into your family? These are the questions that are on the lips of every family, the topic of every talk show, the grist for magazine gossip. Well, perhaps not. But perhaps they should be, given how useful this acronym can be.

FIG TESPN is our way of speaking about the steps adults and children can take to go from ideas to responsible, thoughtful action. FIG TESPN is a model for parents and children to use in solving problems. The name is an acronym for the steps to take in working out those problems; we'll get to what it means in a minute. FIG TESPN is also for use informally with children, to guide parents both in modeling for and asking questions of children that put them on a positive path to sound decision-making and follow-through. Finally, it has some potential use formally by children, but this is not typical for families (it is much more likely to be used this way in schools).

After you have begun creating a more harmonious, caring, and thoughtful family, you can begin to work on facilitating more responsible action grounded in your family's moral framework. Do not worry if things are not perfect yet. First of all, perfection does not exist; parenting needs to be viewed as an ongoing process. You will need to keep doing all the things from the previous chapters with greater or lesser intensity, but you are now ready to add a problem-solving process to the mix.

It is important to remember that problem-solving occurs in the context of relationships and values. Children can be resistant to talking with parents about a problem because they feel criticized and, therefore, become defensive. People get defensive when they perceive an attack. Often, parents think they are helping children be aware of a problem so they can solve it, but the child thinks they are being criticized on top of already feeling bad about what they did. The child becomes defensive, denies guilt, and the more the parent pushes, the more defensive the child becomes. This usually escalates to the point of an argument, rather than the discussion the parent had hoped for.

Emotional Intelligence Principles Highlighted in This Chapter's Activities

☞ 1. Be Aware of One's Own Feelings and Those of Others
  2. Show Empathy and Understand Others' Points of View
  3. Regulate and Cope Positively with Emotional and Behavioral Impulses
☞ 4. Be Positive Goal- and Plan-Oriented
☞ 5. Use Positive Social Skills in Handling Relationships

The emphasis on feelings, goals, plans, and skills is our way of tying together the need to keep our feelings, thoughts, and actions coordinated for effective problem-solving in the real world. Emotionally Intelligent Parenting is, above all, realistic. There is no point to making things artificially simple, or to have great ideas and discussions without thinking through how to actually carry them out. Let's look at an example that shows how we put FIG TESPN into action, and then we will explain it in detail.

A family came to one of our offices for therapy because their fifteen-year-old son had stolen money from a close family friend. The parents were embarrassed, angry, and concerned about their adolescent. When they spoke to him, at first he denied it, then, when confronted with the evidence, casually admitted to the theft without expression of remorse. This outraged the parents even more and led to a spiraling conflict.

But what was really going on here? Did the parents do such a bad job that they had raised a sociopath without a sense of right and wrong, without the capacity for guilt? Often parents react to a child as if they really were bad parents who had instilled no values or conscience in their children, and had raised a serial killer.

You need to have confidence in yourself as a parent. When your child has made an error in judgment, no matter how egregious, chances are good that it is not evidence of major psychopathology that only years of therapy, medication, and residential placement at a clinic far from home will cure (even if you want to send him there). You need to view it as a "mistake." It is rare that parents have not instilled in their children the proper values, but the nature of the relationship between parent and child will affect the expression of those values.

In the present example, as the conflict between parent and child grew, the child became more defensive and the parent became more offensive. What was needed was a way for parent and child to discuss the problem and for both parties to decide what to do. The parents needed to be aware of their own feelings and to decide what they should do, and their son needed to be aware of his feelings and decide what he should do. All the therapist did in this case was to guide the family through this process. But luckily for you, we are now giving this process away as a special bonus for buying this book. We hope it will save you expensive years of therapy.

As mentioned earlier, FIG TESPN is an acronym for problem-solving, decision-making, and action-planning. It is important to view this as a process, not as a formula. It is okay if you start in the middle, work backwards from the end to the beginning, or take it sequentially, step by step. Sometimes you will do part of it, sometimes all of it. With younger children you may do more of it; older children will do more of it on their own. You will learn an abridged version when pressured for time, and an expanded version for working on serious life issues.

When you are using FIG TESPN to facilitate problem-solving, you can keep it in the back of your mind. When you are teaching it to your child to use independently, we recommend that you tell the child who FIG TESPN is. FIG TESPN is like Jiminy Cricket from Disney's *Pinocchio*, or like a sports coach. Jiminy whispered in Pinocchio's ear, but Pinocchio still had to decide what to do. A coach teaches you how to play the game, but stays on the sidelines while you make the on-field decisions and actually play the game. FIG TESPN gives you a way to play the game of life successfully.

As you can see below, this is a complex set of skills. Similar in use to the Keep Calm prompt, FIG TESPN is first modeled by the parent, taught to the child, prompted by the parent, and then used by children independently. It then becomes the prompt or reminder for the child to use the skills.

Rather than being a set of eight discrete steps to problem-solving, FIG TESPN is taught and used as a whole process. It is through the repetition of the whole that the skills embedded within it are learned without losing the overall purpose of solving the child's problem. Each time the process is repeated, a sub-skill (such as identification of feelings, goal-setting, or role-playing assertive behaviors) can be highlighted and reviewed. As much as possible, the child is responsible for generating the ideas that will be used in the process. It is important for the parent to keep in mind that the overall goal is to develop children's independent and responsible problem-solving. Here's what FIG TESPN means:

1. Feelings cue me to thoughtful action.
2. I have a problem.

3. Goal gives me a guide.

4. Think of things I can do.

5. Envision outcomes.

6. Select my best solution.

7. Plan the procedure, anticipate pitfalls, practice, and pursue it.

8. Notice what happened, and now what?

The following are some of the important features of each FIG TESPN problem-solving step.

FEELINGS CUE ME TO THOUGHTFUL ACTION

Feelings are the first step in problem-solving because they let you know that something needs to be done. If we did not feel bad, we would not have a problem. However, when children have bad feelings, they tend to get stuck in those feelings and become immobilized or act out inappropriately. They usually view the bad feeling as the end of the story. FIG TESPN teaches them to use these feelings not as an end result of some unpleasant event, but as a beginning to help them get what they want. A useful analogy is physical pain. If someone got a cut and it did not hurt, they might not notice and could bleed to death. The pain from the cut lets them know that there is a problem and they need to do something to take care of it. If they do not take care of this problem, then things will probably get worse. Bad feelings work the same way. Being upset lets you know that there is a problem that needs to be solved and that if you do not solve it, it will most likely get worse. By using feelings as the cue to thoughtful action, the bad feelings are reframed and children become empowered to act.

It is important to be aware of feelings and identify them. Children's feelings have on-off rather than dimmer switches. They are either good or bad, happy or sad, satiated or starving. It is necessary for them to learn the full range of emotions in between the extremes, and to differentiate those feelings. For example, children often do not make distinctions between disappointment and anger. By learning to label different feelings, children are led to different courses of action. You do not do the same things when you are disappointed that you do when you are angry. Learning to label feelings accurately is called developing a feelings vocabulary, as discussed previously.

I HAVE A PROBLEM

This does not mean that the problem was the child's *fault* (even if it was), but it does mean that it is the child's responsibility to solve it. It is fruitless to try to get a child to admit blame. Admission of guilt is not the point here. The point is to get the child to understand that he is the one who is feeling upset, and therefore he is the one who has to solve the problem. The child can talk all he wants about why the problem was not his fault, but this will not solve the problem. Children often externalize blame and thereby externalize responsibility for solving the problem. This then leaves the child powerless to work on the problem because of his focus on what others need to do. The purpose of this step in problem-solving is not to ascribe blame but to have the child accept responsibility for solving it and to put the problem into words, which is the first step. Another important point here is that problems cannot be solved with *feelings;* you can only think your way to appropriate *actions.* Having children verbalize a problem is another way to foster impulse control. If you are thinking and talking, you are likely not acting yet.

It is difficult to identify the problem and sort it out from various other problems or feelings that may be occurring simultaneously. At this point, if children come up with problems that seem irrelevant to the situation, you can do one of two things: by using the "Columbo" Technique, you can question how what they are saying relates to the feeling they were initially talking about, or you can allow them to continue with subsequent steps. At some point they may see that their solution does not address the problem as stated. At that point, go back and reformulate the problem. It is also possible that the child's new problem is the real problem that was bothering her.

For example, two children had a fight. The parent asks what the problem is. One child says that the problem is that John is a jerk. If the child then attempts to develop options to deal with this, he may see that regardless of what he does, he can't be sure that he will make John less of a jerk. Also, these solutions will tend to rely on John doing a lot of things that John has yet to do, which sounds a lot more like wishful thinking than smart problem-solving. At some point you may help the child reformulate the problem in a way that has the word *I* in it, such as "I don't like it when John keeps teasing me," or "When John teases me, I feel bad [or mad, etc.]."

GOAL GIVES ME A GUIDE

Among the most important parts of FIG TESPN is the *G*: "Goal gives me a guide." Many children today lack focus, direction, motivation. Many parents feel concern about children's poor use of time—both in academics and leisure. What too often is not recognized is that goal-setting is a skill, and therefore one that can be taught. Once learned, it will be used because it is a proven stress-reliever.

For example, when many of us have a lot to do, and we are feeling a bit overwhelmed, what is a natural thing to do? Make a list! And what is making a list? A goal-setting activity to guide our next actions. Once we have a list, there is a tendency to feel better, to feel a sense of relief. Indeed, this is so true that many of us take a break after we make our lists—even though we have not actually made a dent in our workload. We will show you how, in the course of everyday activities ranging from going out to dinner to managing the morning routine to dealing with homework and extracurricular demands, you can build your children's goal-setting and self-guidance skills.

A goal is a thing one wants to have happen. It can be thought of as a problem upside down: the problem is I handed my homework in late; my goal is to hand my homework in on time. Without goals, we have no direction.

Children need to understand that goals give us direction for our actions so that we can achieve what we really want. It is also important for children to learn how to set reasonable and attainable goals. This will occur over time as children practice this process. It is also necessary to identify subgoals and to prioritize goals. For example, a goal may be to be popular. Subgoals under this are to be cool and hang out with friends, but also to get good grades and a good job, and earn good money (this too can make one popular). Obviously, these subgoals can conflict. Being aware of them can help a child learn to delay gratification, and discussing them can be a worthwhile activity in itself.

By the way, earlier, when we discussed the idea of writing a Family Mission Statement, we were anticipating this discussion of goals. Mission statements are big things in companies right now, to give companies cohesive direction, so that everyone from the evening security guard to the CEO knows what the company stands for and where it is going. A Family Mission Statement serves the same purpose. It is both a statement of values and over-all goals of the family. If you have not yet done so, then perhaps now would be a good time to consider it seriously.

Think of Things I Can Do

Oh, if only there were a magic wand that a parent could tap on a child's head to get him to think. Usually the wand commonly used to get children to think borders on child abuse, and just gets them to think that their parent hates them. At this step in the process we have a modest goal: to get the child to think of as many different things to do as she can, without judging any ideas as good or bad. One of the beauties of FIG TESPN is that it breaks down an extremely complex process into concrete, manageable parts that can be taught directly and mastered. How many times have you asked rhetorically, "Why don't you think before you do something?" FIG TESPN teaches the child how to do this, rather than assuming that he can.

By teaching children to think before they act, we are teaching impulse control. We also want to teach children to think in a creative, expansive manner. This has been called "thinking outside the box." This is done through a brainstorming process in which critical judgment is suspended. It is important that neither parent nor child censors thought, because this cuts off creative thinking. Sometimes a silly idea helps you think of a good idea. For example, you and your child are thinking of ways to make more friends. The child suggests he could pay other children to be his friend. This makes you think about having a bowling party for some of the children.

It is important to think of as many things as possible. As you go through the process, you can refine or combine some of them. For younger or resistant children, the parent may need to offer more suggestions, but this is okay. After some training, children can get pretty good at this. The more potential solutions you generate, the better chance you have of getting what you want. Life is complex, and there is rarely one right answer to a problem.

ENVISION OUTCOMES

In addition to a magic wand, wouldn't it be great to have a crystal ball? We could gaze into it to see what will happen. Sometimes we think we're in the wrong profession and should open up a psychic parenting hotline. But until we do, you will have to teach children to envision the future for themselves. This involves getting them to think about what might happen before they do something. Wouldn't that be great! It's unfortunate that you cannot just expect it or demand it, but have to teach it. You do this by asking, explaining, and practicing. You help children see the consequences of past actions (remember "Stuff Happens"?), help them think about what will happen when doing a FIG TESPN, and reinforce them for making good choices when they do (praise).

After the child has thought of things he can do to solve the problem, it is necessary for him to envision what would happen if he tried out his ideas. The word *envision* was chosen carefully for its connotation of *seeing*. It is helpful if children are able to picture outcomes to themselves, not just think about them. "Envisioning" can happen after each option is conceived (especially for younger children), or you can wait until the whole list is generated. When presenting this phase to children, you need to review the importance of anticipating the consequences of actions. Children need to see that for every action there is a consequence. You can make a game of this by suggesting an action and having the child think of a consequence. For example, the action is "share toys," the consequence is _____; the action is "fight with your brother," the consequence is _____.

It is necessary to encourage envisioning several outcomes when appropriate. A child may envision that if he hits, the other person may stop bothering him but may also try to get him back, and that the child might then get in trouble with adults for hitting. It will often be necessary for the parent to add potential outcomes that were unforeseen by the child.

SELECT MY BEST SOLUTION

If you have gotten this far, your child has probably forgotten why you are doing a FIG TESPN. You may have too. You need to refer back to the original problem and goal. Children are easily distracted and are expert at distracting their parents, especially when talking about their problems. Usually, off-topic comments are best ignored, especially those designed to provoke. Remind them of what they said they wanted. Make sure that the solution addresses this. It may be necessary to rethink one or several of the previous steps. When formulating a solution, several options can be combined. For example, where the goal is to pass a test, the solution may be for the child to develop a study schedule, ask a friend to study with him, and outline all of the chapters.

PLAN THE PROCEDURE, ANTICIPATE PITFALLS, PRACTICE, AND PURSUE IT

This is a pretty big step. If children—or adults—could just do this step of the process, they would be highly socially competent. Planning does not come as naturally as impulsive behavior, because of the influence of emotions. However, as we have been stating throughout this book, these skills can be taught.

Planning needs to be presented to children as a way of giving them a better chance to get what they want. For example, if a child wants to have a sleep-over, she could just call some friends to come over that night, or she could plan out who will come, when they will come, what they will do, where they will sleep, and how she will ask her parents. When presenting the concept of planning to children, adult analogies can be used, such as planning to buy a car versus buying the first one you see, or planning a vacation versus just getting in the car and driving.

Anticipating pitfalls or obstacles to the plan helps prevent frustration and failure. By thinking ahead about what could happen that would prevent them from implementing their plan, your children are preparing ahead of time for these pitfalls. This also reduces impulsivity.

As with any skill, new or old, it is necessary to practice. Social skills are mastered by doing them. But instead of throwing children into the ocean to practice swimming, we have them role-play. It is necessary to make actions as concrete and true to life as possible in order for children to genuinely use them in the real world. Children may be able to say they will do something, but then do not really know how to do it, or do it inappropriately. Also, having them act it out enables the parent to see other skills that children may lack, such as assertive communication, or anger control that may need to be reviewed (use of BEST, Keep Calm, etc.).

"Pursue it" means that the child has to make the public commitment to do something and to go out and try it. The child also needs to be specific about when he is going to do it. It is not enough to know what to do and how to solve the problem; without a commitment to try, there is less chance that the child really will.

NOTICE WHAT HAPPENED, AND NOW WHAT?

It is important for the parent to follow up with the child on what happened when she put her plan into effect. This serves two purposes: first, the child knows you take her problems seriously; and second, it encourages the child to self-evaluate. How does the child feel now about the situation? Did the plan work? Were there unanticipated obstacles? Was the goal what she really wanted?

Another aspect of problem-solving is for children to understand that despite their best efforts, their plans might not meet with success. As adults, we know that this is how life is. Social dynamics are so complicated that it is impossible to have the perfect solution all the time. All we can do is our best. If children understand this from the start, it makes them less vulnerable to disappointment. It may be necessary to rethink the problem or decision, and engage in another FIG TESPN, using the result of the initial FIG TESPN as the problem to be solved. Make sure to start with the feelings about not having solved the problem or not having the decision work out.

APPLICATIONS OF FIG TESPN TO EVERYDAY LIFE

There are three applications of FIG TESPN to family life. The first is for parents when doing their own problem-solving. We have given you a lot of strategies to use, and it is not easy to figure out what to do, and when. For example, you may be riding in the car, listening to your kids fighting in the backseat. You can do a quick FIG TESPN for yourself:

F —angry, tired
I —kids fighting
G—want them to get along
T—pull over for a "time out"
  —yell
  —threaten to take something away
  —ask what the problem is
E —too dangerous
  —I'll feel bad
  —hear whining
  —solve the problem?
S —ask what the problem is
P—Keep Calm, ask in an even tone, ask each one to speak separately
N—if this does not work, threaten no dessert after dinner and deal with the whining

TIPS FOR PARENTS IN PROBING CHILDREN FOR MORE RESPONSIBLE DECISION-MAKING AND ACTION

The second application is to guide children through the FIG TESPN process, encouraging them to arrive at their own thoughtful action without formally introducing FIG TESPN. You can do this in a more spontaneous manner than FIG TESPN. At the end of this chapter, we provide a series of sample questions to ask at each step. The questioning can really start at any step, depending on the situation. Sometimes you will want to start at "I" to get a sense of what the problem is about before you talk about feelings. At other times you may discuss what the child did to solve a problem (the "S" and "P" phases), and then work your way back to the feelings, problem, goal, and other options available (the "T" phase). You want to think of this as a process, rather than a sequence to be followed in a lockstep manner. When doing this, remember to use the Guiding Principles. Patience and persistence are especially important when a child responds, "I don't know."

GENERAL TIPS

Start slowly and patiently. Judge your child's tolerance for having to do a lot of thinking and for dealing with your questions. For some kids who are not used to this kind of thinking, it may be mentally tiring; don't think they are just avoiding your efforts if they protest at first. Gradually move them through all the steps, or just concentrate on the areas you think are especially important for a particular situation.

QUESTION-BY-QUESTION TIPS

F Be sure children use "feeling" words rather than descriptions of the problem or what they did. You may have to prompt by suggesting feelings (Did you feel nervous? Did you feel your Feelings Fingerprint in your stomach? Did your face get all red?) This can be difficult, but it is important for the child to learn.

I   Be sure to encourage specifics and make sure you understand the sequence of events and actions: who did what, and when.

G   Have children focus on what they want, not on what they want to do, or want others to do, but the endpoint, the final result, when things are all over and resolved. Remember not to direct the goal yourself. Take care here, as children may have a hard time telling the difference between between a goal and something they can do to achieve that goal.

T   When generating different options, ask what they have already tried. This gives them credit for trying to think about the situation independently. It also gives you a chance to see what kind of thinking your children are doing on their own. After this, have the child brainstorm as many things as possible. Do not critique at this point; hard as it may be, just listen and encourage more ideas. The more ideas you can get out, say four or five, the better the quality of the action your children eventually will choose.

E   Review each option; sometimes it is useful to write these down to keep track of them. Have children anticipate the potential outcomes, using the language of pictures and imagery to help them make this more vivid and real. Again, you may want to write this down, just as if you were diagramming a sentence. You can show different possible results of various solutions. Different lines can stand for long-term and short-term results, and consequences for the children and for others involved. After you have probed a bit, you may want to add likely outcomes that you are aware of, but that your children may not have thought about.

S   The point of a solution is to reach a goal. Remind children of the goal, and ask if this will enable them to achieve the goal.

P   Review who, what, where, and how. Detail is critical in making a responsible, thoughtful plan and having a good chance for success. Anticipate problems in implementing the plan and how the child can deal with these. Through role-playing practice, the social skills needed to put a good idea into action can be taught, enabling children to implement a plan more successfully. Have the child make a commitment to try the plan. Prepare the child for potential frustration in achieving the goal. Have them think about what they would do then, including repeating the FIG TESPN process. This may need to be bypassed for younger children because it requires a relatively high level of cognitive sophistication.

N   After implementation of the child's plan, review with the child what she did or did not do. Do not get discouraged if she did not use the plan. Follow-up will be extremely important: it reinforces children for problem-solving, helps them adapt the plan as necessary, and lets them know you really care about them.

ONE FATHER'S FIG TESPN STORY

One of the authors combined FIG TESPN and Keep Calm to handle a volatile situation with his daughter. The story provides a good example of these techniques in action.

My daughter, who is nine, has been enrolled in a recreational day camp for the past couple of summers. The three-week session culminates in a play or skit that the campers have put together, performed for the parents. My daughter has always had a great deal of input into the productions, and has had a chance to do some of the choreography and select some of the music used in the production. This year she had her heart set on doing a skit based around some of the music from the Broadway musical *Annie*. When she got to camp, however, she learned that some of the other kids wanted to do a skit based on the movie *Space Jam*. So the kids took a vote and decided to select the music from *Space Jam*. My daughter came home very upset that day, and the following discussion ensued:

DAD: How was camp today?

DAUGHTER: I'd rather not talk about it!

DAD: No, c'mon, how was camp today?

DAUGHTER: Well, it didn't go real well.

DAD: What do you mean by that?

DAUGHTER: Well, all the kids couldn't decide on a skit to put on, and I really wanted to use the music from *Annie*, but no one else wanted to use it except for another girl in my group, so they took a vote and the majority of the kids wanted to use songs and music from *Space Jam*, which is really awful. I really don't like the music at all.

DAD: How were you feeling when that happened? [Let's find out how she was feeling.]

DAUGHTER: I was mad and upset.

DAD: Is that all you were feeling? [Rephrasing gets at more feelings.]

DAUGHTER: Well, I was also feeling very frustrated and disappointed. I was looking forward to doing this for a long time.

DAD: Yeah, I guess it's hard to count on doing something and then it doesn't work out. Now, what are you going to do?

DAUGHTER: Well, I decided that I'm not going to participate in the show!

DAD: Let's take a look at this situation a little differently.

DAUGHTER: What do you mean?

DAD: I was wondering if you could tell me in your words what you think the problem is? [Here, we are defining the problem.]

DAUGHTER: Well, the other kids don't want to use the music from *Annie* that I suggested. That's it, and I'm upset.

DAD: Is that all?

DAUGHTER: Well, I really had my heart set on using the music so then I could have had a lead role and sung one of my favorite songs, "Tomorrow."

DAD: Oh, so you really wanted to be in the limelight.

DAUGHTER: I guess the problem is that I wanted to sing the song and be a lead in the show! [Now we get to the heart of the problem.]

DAD: Well, there's nothing wrong with that. But sometimes other kids have to have the opportunity to have a lead role in the play. Okay, now that you know what the problem is, let's figure out some goals for you—even though you don't want to be in the show. [Prompting for goals.]

DAUGHTER: What do you mean by that?

DAD: Well, even though you don't have a lead in the show, are there are still some things you would like to see happen with the show?

DAUGHTER: You know, I would have never thought about that! I guess one of my goals could be to see that the set is designed right and the dancing looks good.

DAD: There you have it! Now let's look at some things you could do! Let's brainstorm! [Think of as many ideas as possible.]

DAUGHTER: Okay! I guess I could ask my counselor if I could help paint the set, or help with the choreography or even be an assistant director.

DAD: Wow! You really came up with some great ideas! Now let's picture some of those ideas. For instance, what do you see happening if you decide to help with the set?

DAUGHTER: I guess if I helped with the set, I could see the other kids really appreciating my artistic abilities and they would be happy that I was helping.

DAD: Great going! How about the choreography? [Encourage envisioning of outcomes.]

DAUGHTER: Well, I've taken a lot of dance classes and I guess the kids and the counselors would like it if I helped them stage the movements to the various dances.

DAD: How about being an assistant director?

DAUGHTER: Well...I'm not sure.

DAD: What do you mean?

DAUGHTER: Well, I could see that it would be fun being an assistant to the director, but I'm afraid the other kids might not listen to me.

DAD: I see what you mean. Well, which idea to you think is the best solution for you? [Selecting her best solution.]

DAUGHTER: I think I'd like to help with the choreography. That way I could be part of the fun and help the other kids with the show.

DAD: Sounds good, but how are you going to approach the other kids and the staff? [Plan it!]

DAUGHTER: Maybe tomorrow I could approach my counselor and share with him my idea to help out.

DAD: When do you think it would be best to approach your counselor?

DAUGHTER: I think that when you drop me off, before everyone comes to camp, I could speak to him about my idea. I might be a little nervous, you know!

DAD: Remember that you can always use the Keep Calm strategy that I taught you before you share your idea with your counselor.

DAUGHTER: That's a good idea, Dad, maybe I'll practice the Keep Calm strategy now, and rehearse with you what I would say.

DAD: What a great idea!

DAUGHTER: Okay, so now that I'm calmed down, I can ask my counselor politely if I could help with the choreography.

DAD: How do you feel now?

DAUGHTER: I feel better about camp.

DAD: Great! Tomorrow you can try out your plan, and then we can see how things turned out. [Notice what happens next and get ready to follow up.]

DAUGHTER: Thanks, Dad!

By using simple probes and questions and following the FIG TESPN approach, it was possible for me to help my daughter work through this problem. The more parents encourage their children to use FIG TESPN, the more likely it is that the children will internalize the steps and begin to use them spontaneously as they get older.

FORMAL FIG TESPNING

The third application is to formally teach FIG TESPN and use it as a guide for dealing with problems and helping children develop more thoughtful actions. For this more formal and structured application, you should first review who FIG TESPN is, using the Jiminy Cricket or sports-coach analogy. Then talk about how this can help the child solve problems and get what he wants. After this, review each letter, using concept highlights and examples. Then tell him you will be practicing and using FIG TESPN in different ways.

As soon as possible after introducing FIG TESPN, get a videotape of a television sitcom or a family movie. Watch the video with the child and use FIG TESPN as a guide to discuss the characters' feelings, problems, goals, and so on. Use the "pause" button when necessary. When talking about feelings, focus on nonverbal cues such as facial expressions and body postures. When talking about thinking of things to do, identify what the characters chose to do and have your child think of alternatives. The videotape should give you lots of opportunities to envision outcomes.

In some ways, in terms of values, the worse the video, the better. Some cartoon shows, for example, can be viewed critically with the use of FIG TESPN. Old sitcoms with sexist stereotypes (*I Love Lucy* is an example) are also useful for making a distinction between how the television characters handle problems and how your family does. Using FIG TESPN while watching television helps children become active, critical viewers of media rather than passively accepting others' values and ways of behavior. When you watch television in this manner, even you will be surprised at the inappropriate role-modeling that goes on in "family" shows.

While watching television with your children and FIG TESPN, you can emphasize a particular letter. You can tell the kids, for example, that today you are going to find as many "goals" as you can. This lends itself to more focused viewing. You can discuss long- and short-term goals and the problem of conflicting goals.

OTHER FAMILY FIG TESPN TIMES

You can use FIG TESPN, either formally or informally, when you are:

- discussing current events around the dinner table
- planning family activities such as vacations
- making family decisions
- resolving sibling conflicts
- reviewing education and career issues
- talking about persistent problems
- responding to a crisis

1. Current events discussion

This is something you may want to share with your children's teachers. Actually, we are bringing it to you based on many years of successful use in schools of all kinds. Children's understanding of current events—whether from newspapers, magazines, television, or radio—benefits from some focused discussion. FIG TESPN provides a way for your children to think about world, state, and local events—and even school events—in a way that brings them to life, exercises children's problem-solving skills, and prepares them for responsible action.

In any given story, usually there are different people making decisions about critical events. Who are those people or groups? What are their goals? How are they feeling about the current situation? What might they do? How might different possibilities work out? Will they reach their goals? And what about your children—what are their feelings about the issue? Are there things they might like to do?

Asking your kids questions like these brings them into current events and opens up the possibility that they might take action. Among many examples we have seen are a group of teens inspired by FIG TESPN to plan a teen center, a group of middle-school students who helped their town develop a way to collect and recycle plastics, a group of teens who decided that a good way to help the elderly be less afraid of them would be to organize themselves to assist seniors with walking around town, shopping, raking leaves, and shoveling snow, and individual students who wrote letters and sent E-mails to public officials and school officials about things that concerned them. You will be pleasantly surprised at how, with FIG TESPN questions you ask as an initial guide, your children become more alert, thoughtful, and active around current events.

2. *Family event planning*

Is there a party coming up? How about a vacation? Don't settle—give FIG TESPN a chance to help out. Actually, it's the TESPN part that will be of most value. Have everyone brainstorm a variety of possibilities. But don't just jump into it. First do a couple of mind-clearing, brain-activating activities. For example, what could this figure be?

\\\\\\///////\\\\\\\////

Have everyone in the family take a look at this picture. Then let everyone shout out their ideas about what it could be. Give yourselves two minutes, and have someone write all the ideas down. *Remember the rules of brainstorming: No judgments about what others have said, no criticisms; nothing can be too silly, and nothing can be "wrong."*

Do the same procedure with this figure:

œœœœ

Or try this one:

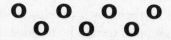

Then take a household object—for example a spoon, a ruler, a frying pan, a sponge, a pen, a pillow, an aluminum cooking tin— and have everyone take turns saying what they think it could be used for, or could be, other than what it obviously is. For example, a frying pan might be a helmet, a tennis racquet, something for making crêpes, a plow, a mallet used to try to win a prize at a county fair, a home for frogs, a vacuum cleaner—you get the idea. People can just say what comes to mind, or you can pass the object around and people can take turns, passing if they want to.

This kind of activity loosens up people's thinking, helps them become more creative, so that when it comes time for planning a family event, new ideas or creative combinations of several ideas are more likely to emerge.

3. Family decision-making

This is an extension of ideas we have already described, but it focuses on something that many families have a hard time with— actually making a choice. Here, FIG TESPN gives us important guiding questions: What is our goal? Which ideas can help us reach that goal? Of these, which ones can we actually carry out according to a plan? Then, the final question: Do we really *want* to reach our goal? If the answer is yes, then FIG TESPN usually will lead us to a decision. If the answer is no, then FIG TESPN cannot help you; only you can decide what your goals are.

4. Sibling conflicts

The kids are yelling, pushing, maybe hitting each other. Certainly there is conflict. Like Jiminy Cricket, FIG TESPN is always on hand to help you handle things in a way that builds children's emotional intelligence skills. FIG TESPN helps clarify what people are feeling and thinking. First, separate the children. You are going to want to establish what happened, but don't get too hung up on it; the truth in these matters can be hard to find. Ask the older child what she wanted to have happen with regard to her sibling. Did she want to play? Get something? Just mind her own business? Ask a question? What brought them together? Then ask the younger child the same type of questions. Next, ask the older sibling if the conflict was helping her get what she wants. (Here you are using both FIG TESPN and the Guiding Principles.)

5. Education and career guidance

In the education and career area, a special use of FIG TESPN involves focusing on the last two steps: plan the procedure, anticipate pitfalls, practice, and pursue it, and notice what happened and figure out what should happen next. There is a gap between a good idea and putting it into action in a responsible manner.

"I'm gonna study and get good grades."

"That's terrific. I'm so glad to hear it! Tell me, when do you plan on studying?"

"Oh, later."

"When is your test?"

"Day after tomorrow."

"Where will you do your studying?"

"In the library, I guess. I'll go after school tomorrow."

"Well, let's take a look at what's going on. Tomorrow after school you have the A/V Club meeting. Can you miss that?"

"No, or I won't get credit."

"So how does this affect your studying plan?"

"It, uhh, I, uhh, will have to study today, I guess."

Here the parent's job is to help the child think through the details of carrying out what is a terrific idea. We know a lot about the real world, about how to actually get things done, that kids are still learning. By gently guiding them to think through these situations, we impart some of our wisdom to them, and gradually we will see their own skills grow. The first place you are likely to see progress in this area is when kids begin to self-criticize, realizing even before you say something that their plans might need some modifying. Planning skills, including being ready for roadblocks if they are encountered, form the bridge to responsible action.

In a career-planning context, FIG TESPN is a guide for interview preparation, among other areas. What are you going to say? How will you say it? What will you say when they ask why you want the job, what you plan to be doing five years from now, what you have to bring to this company that is special, and so on? Role-play exactly how your child will respond, focusing on one's BEST skills and the use of Keep Calm before and even during an interview. The step of "Notice what happened" refers to the process of "debriefing" after an interview. What happened? What do I think went best? What might have gone better? What was unexpected? How might I handle that if it comes up again? What else do I want to take with me for the next interview? These are questions one can ask oneself, or that parents can help their child think about during their post-interview conversations.

6. Persistent family conflicts

Applications of FIG TESPN to persistent family conflicts range from using FIG TESPN as a way of getting families out of a "rut" to its use in clinical settings, as we do in our work as psychologists. FIG TESPN doesn't change in these different situations; rather, it's often the case that clinical situations are more emotionally charged and one of the major jobs of the clinician is to help family members focus on the conflict at hand and stick with their application of FIG TESPN, as well as other skills that may need to be taught.

To help "unstick" persistent patterns of conflict, a family member—and we like to empower both kids and adults to do this—could call a Family Meeting. If your family already has been using

Sharing Time and some of the other ideas we have mentioned, then such a meeting would be a natural occurrence and, as we call it technically, "no big deal." If you are trying to have this kind of meeting for the first time, we suggest you use Keep Calm on yourself before, during, and after such a meeting. The approach we recommend for the convener is to borrow from the Columbo Technique and indicate that he is puzzled about how to address the particular issue (such as chores not getting done, too much yelling or hitting in the house, too many put-downs, not enough time together, kids doing poorly in school and resisting parental guidance for improvement, rooms being a mess, two family members engaged in verbal warfare and other hostilities, divorced parents disagreeing or being inconsistent). "I would like everyone's help, so can we please all sit down for a few minutes together on Sunday night at about eight [or some other time that is likely to be convenient for everyone] and talk about this?" At the meeting, it might be helpful to take out the Family Problem-Solving Worksheet at the end of the chapter. The worksheet lays out a series of steps based on FIG TESPN, and encourages everyone to contribute their ideas. Once ideas are on the table, FIG TESPN can be used to put the problem into words, set a goal, and brainstorm lots of possible solutions.

7. Responding to a crisis

In a pinch, FIG TESPN can be used to clarify matters and move everyone involved toward responsible action. Crises might include a child getting sick in the middle of the night, a badly scraped knee after a bicycle spill, a big fight with a friend, leaving one's math book in school the day before a math test, or a disagreement with one's spouse over how to spend the Christmas bonus. You can use all or parts of FIG TESPN to help sort out your own feelings and take prompt, effective action when in crisis mode. Here are the key elements of FIG TESPN that can be used when the nature of the crisis does not allow for the full treatment or when someone is having a FIT (we just love acronyms!):

F Feelings are your cue to problem-solve. Be aware of your feelings and those of others. Do Keep Calm, and encourage others to do it as well.

I I have a problem and need a goal. Figure out what is happening and what most needs to happen next.

T Think of things to do. Itemize main options quickly and think through what is most feasible and how to carry it out. Get moving and keep track of what is happening to make sure the problem is being solved.

What makes FIG TESPN part of Emotionally Intelligent Parenting is that parents are alert to the fact that in crisis, we risk emotional hijacking. When this happens, responsible action is less likely. So, Emotionally Intelligent Parents prepare for crisis. An index card with the FIT crisis steps is on their refrigerator, in their car, or somewhere else easily accessible, often not far from a phone. Just looking at the card is a source of reassurance, of emotional stability, of confidence that if we use what we know, we will be more likely to work through the crisis than if we panic or let our strong feelings take over. We all have been through crises. We use our skills to look into the future through the lens of the past and envision how we will act when we are in crises in the future. Most of us recognize that with a little structure and an advance plan, we will be able to get through it a little more easily.

A FINAL WORD

FIG TESPN is a powerful tool for Emotionally Intelligent Parenting. Realistically, we will not be using FIG all the time; what happens in households characterized by Emotionally Intelligent Parenting is that FIG TESPN is present in at least a couple of forms. What matters is that you find some ways of using the skills of FIG TESPN comfortably and consistently in your family, in a way that makes most sense to you. In the next chapter we illustrate the most natural way in which parents use FIG TESPN and build up their children's skills for making thoughtful decisions and taking responsible action. This happens through parent-child conversations. You will read a variety of different dialogues between parents and children that happen in the course of every-day events. We will provide some comments so that you can see the patterns involved and try it yourself more easily. Pick and choose the examples most relevant for your family, and then check out some of the others.

FAMILY PROBLEM-SOLVING PLANNER

Date: _____

F We are **feeling**:

I We **identify** our family's problem as:

G Our family's **goal** is:

T Let's **think** of many different things we can do:

_____

_____

_____

_____

E Let's **envision** the outcomes:

_____

_____

_____

S Let's **select** our family's best solution:

_____

_____

P Let's **plan** the procedure, anticipate pitfalls, practice, and pursue it:

_____

N Let's **notice** what happened and what we need to do now:

_____

QUESTIONS TO GUIDE FIG TESPN THINKING

If you want to encourage this kind of thinking in your children:	Use questions like this:
F Feelings cue me to problem-solve.	How are you feeling? How else are you feeling? I notice you seem _____. How do you think _____ is feeling?
I I have a problem.	I would like to know exactly what happened. What happened before this? What were you doing? What was _____ doing? What happened after? What did you do then?
G Goal gives me a guide.	What would you like to have happen? What is your goal?
T Think of things I can do.	What did you try to do? What have you thought of doing? What else can you think of doing?
E Envision outcomes, both short and long term, for the children and for others.	Picture what might happen if you _____? Close your eyes and try to imagine doing what you said you would. What do you see happening? When? What about later? How might it affect you? What about other people? What else could

happen? What might happen
if you _____? You thought
about _____ and _____ as
possibilities. What about
_____ or _____?

S Select my best solution.   Of the things you thought
about, which one seems like
the best thing to try first?
Which one will get you to
your goal?

P Plan the procedure,   How would you do it? What is
anticipate pitfalls, practice,   your plan? Show me what you
and pursue it.   are going to do. Maybe we
can practice this together
before you try it. What if
things do not work out the
way you want? What would
you do then? What else could
you try? What if _____ happened? How would you han-
dle it?

N Notice what happened, and   Okay, think about it and try it.
consider what I will do   When will we talk about what
next.   happened?

Chapter 7

Parent-Child Conversations on Important Education-Related Problems and Choices

■   ■   ■

One of the largest points of agreement among people of all different backgrounds is that they want their children to get a good education. Parents and children face many hazards and choices on the road to completing school. During these times, parents need to truly communicate with their children. And this is not easy. True communication requires listening, questioning, sometimes withholding our own opinions so that we can hear what our children are saying, and making sure we don't automatically take solutions that were right for us in our times and assume they are right for our children in their times.

We must talk to children in a way that keeps the channels of communication open between them and us. Disagreements can be bridged when there is a channel of communication; when there is not, matters can become much more difficult. Up to now, we have presented the principles of Emotionally Intelligent Parenting in different pieces. But in many situations you are going to need to pull them together. Questions that help bring FIG TESPN into family discussions and the Guiding Principles mentioned earlier, especially facilitative questioning, are important to help your children use their thinking and emotional skills to make responsible choices and carry them out effectively.

What follows, then, is a series of examples of parent-child conversations, drawn from actual situations we have dealt with in the schools, in our clinical work, or in our own homes. As you read through them, notice especially how parents work hard to listen, elicit their children's point of view, and don't take over and impose their ideas. Certainly there will be times when you have very strong opinions, and these must be presented to your children. But the time to do so is after you have listened, which may modify exactly what you say and how you say it. Further, when parents engage in genuine dialogue with their children, sometimes they are surprised to learn that their kids' ideas are not so far from their own. By working with your child's ideas, you are much more likely to be successful in getting your children to believe and follow through on what you might think to be best.

The examples we provide in this chapter cover areas related to education because its importance in virtually all households is inescapable. Applying Emotionally Intelligent Parenting to school-related issues leads to many opportunities to help children—and families—grow. Overall topic areas include

- starting a new school and getting used to new kids
- reacting to report cards and progress reports
- homework, and balancing homework with other aspects of family life
- deciding on a career

Emotional Intelligence Principles Highlighted in This Chapter's Activities

☞1. Be Aware of One's Own Feelings and Those of Others
☞2. Show Empathy and Understand Others' Points of View
  3. Regulate and Cope Positively with Emotional and Behavioral Impulses
☞4. Be Positive Goal- and Plan-Oriented
  5. Use Positive Social Skills in Handling Relationships

KICKBALL CRISIS IN ELEMENTARY SCHOOL

The elementary school years are times when children are learning how to make and keep friends, how to share, how to react
when they don't get their way, and lots of other important social
and emotional skills. Let's see how seven-year-old Aramas and her
mom, Ellen, handle a typical situation:

ARAMAS: I hate them. I hate them all!

ELLEN: Hold on a second. You seem really angry. What happened?

ARAMAS: Daniel and Tim and Adam...and Scott and Rebecca,
too. All except Danny.

ELLEN: What about them?

ARAMAS: They all get everyone together to play kickball, and
they're not so good.

ELLEN: You hate them because they're not so good? Or did something else happen?

ARAMAS: Stephanie and me and Danny and Michelle, we were
just standing around. They come over and get everyone
together and go and play kickball. But not us.

ELLEN: It sounds like you felt pretty mad about this.

ARAMAS: I hate them.

ELLEN: Wow. But you know, I'm not exactly sure yet what the
problem is.

ARAMAS: They get to play and we don't. There's only one game at
a time.

ELLEN: So what is it that you want to have happen?

ARAMAS: I want to play kickball and have fun!

ELLEN: Well, I don't blame you. So, what ideas do you have so
that you can play next time?

ARAMAS: I think I may hit Adam if he comes near me.

ELLEN: Well, that is one thing you could do. What else could you
do that would help you to be playing?

ARAMAS: I don't know.

ELLEN: Oh, come on. I know you have good ideas, even when you are mad. Would it help you to use Keep Calm first?

ARAMAS (doesn't answer right away but starts breathing more slowly): I could tell Adam that he's not my friend anymore.

ELLEN: I wonder what else you could do so that you would be able to play. That is what you want, isn't it?

ARAMAS: Yeah, I guess so. Maybe I can get all my good friends and start the game tomorrow and leave them out.

ELLEN: Any other ideas?

ARAMAS: Uhh, I could, uhh, tell the aide or maybe the teacher that Adam isn't being fair.

ELLEN: You sure could do that. I have another idea of what you could do.

ARAMAS: What?

ELLEN: You could ask Adam and especially Tim and Daniel why you weren't picked. I remember, when I was at school, there was a time when some kids started a game and needed only four or five people, and asked some of my friends but not me. I got really mad at my friends who played, but then I spoke to them and found out that they really didn't leave me out. They were asked by somebody else.

ARAMAS: What did you do?

ELLEN: I didn't have FIG TESPN to help me. And you know Grandma Myra, she was all ready to call the principal and make a big deal out of it. Well, I saw one of the boys in the street in the neighborhood later that afternoon, and I asked him what happened and he didn't really hear me, but he said that if I wanted to play kickball tomorrow, I had to be by the fence right at the start of recess. I didn't find out until later exactly what happened, but I knew that I wasn't being left out.

ARAMAS: That's pretty cool!

ELLEN: Listen, I have to go pick up Sara. You'll have to take a ride with me because she's at the JCC and it will take too long to leave you here. How about if we finish talking in the car?

This discussion of course continues, but we can see already how Mom needs to be patient with a young child telling a story of what is going on at school. What are the facts? Where is the truth? These elusive things are almost never discovered. But parents, if they listen very hard and keep asking questions and use Keep Calm themselves, can eventually learn enough to bring the child along in responsible thinking. Here, a potential fight might have been averted by Mom's focusing on the child's goal. And with young children, it can often broaden their point of view to tell a story about your own childhood, perhaps a bit tailored to fit your child's situation and level of understanding, that helps your child see something he or she is likely to feel quite sure about, from a different perspective. Helping put feelings into words, helping your child keep his or her goals in mind, getting your child into the habit of thinking of a few ideas before settling on one, and, more generally, sharing your wisdom about the nature of friendships in elementary school, all are parenting activities that help build a solid foundation of emotional intelligence for children.

ENCOURAGING EXPRESSION OF FEELINGS

By encouraging children to express their feelings, we show that we are sensitive to the signals they are sending, and that talking about feelings is a good thing to do. This is not a message that all cultures, and families within cultures, necessarily agree with. But Daniel Goleman's work on emotional intelligence makes it clear that feelings are a part of us. They cannot be suppressed, ignored, or put aside. Our feelings influence our actions, and when they are not dealt with at all, we cannot be sure how they will influence what we think, say, or do. As all parents know, sometimes you say things that are different from what you feel in your heart. This is a part of being human. But when it happens consistently, the theory of emotional intelligence warns us there could be trouble ahead, even if it is years down the road, when children finally break away from their parents' watchful eyes.

So, if your culture or belief system is such that expression of feelings is unusual, here is what we suggest from our experience. Don't think about trying to become Leo Buscaglia or Deepak Chopra or Barney or any other very feelings-oriented beings immediately. Think about allowing a little more expression of feelings than you do now. Shift the balance a little, to start with. Sometimes we have found that the mom or the dad is more of a "natural" at this. At those times it is fine for one of you to start and the other to observe, to help begin to get comfortable with the idea of it and how to do it. As a starting point, though, there is no reason why *any* parent should not get better at noticing upset or other troubled feelings in their children. Here are some signs you can look out for that might suggest you follow up on your children's feelings:

- Feelings Fingerprints they display
- words they say
- changes in their routines—sudden stalling around bedtime, getting ready for school, changes in eating or sleeping patterns or energy levels

PROMPTS TO ENCOURAGE EXPRESSION OF FEELINGS

- "How are you feeling? I mean, how are you *really* feeling?"
- "You seem [unhappy, upset, worried, etc., as appropriate]."
- "When I feel sad, I sometimes don't feel like eating, either."
- "What seems to be the matter...I would really like to know."
- "It seems as if something is bothering you. You aren't acting like you usually do. I'd like to talk with you about it."
- "When I see [describe what the child is doing that has alerted you to a possible problem], I know something is the matter. Sometimes it means that [say what you think it might mean], but I'm not sure. Am I right, or is it something else?"

Any of the above probes, and many others, can be used to elicit your child's feelings. If your child resists, don't push too hard. If it is a serious issue, the feeling will be there for another attempt. Just be sure to let your child know that you are available if he or she wants to talk. And sometimes it can mean a lot to say not much at all, but just give your child a gentle touch or a hug. There is no better way to say "I care about you."

RESPOND TO WHAT YOU HEAR WITH ACCEPTANCE AND ACKNOWLEDGMENT

Note that we did not say "agreement" with what you hear, and as parents we know that sometimes it is not even possible to really understand what you are hearing. But your children's feelings are not right or wrong. Especially when children are young, they may not be very skillful at putting what they feel into words. This process requires our help and coaching. And we certainly do not want them to trust us by sharing their feelings and then to somehow feel as if they were betrayed or put down. Consider this example:

FATHER: John, what seems to be the matter?

JOHN: Nothin'.

FATHER: Really, son, I'd like to know. You haven't been eating lunch, and that's not like you at all.

JOHN: Well, it's Gary. I don't think he likes me anymore, and I'm worried.

FATHER: That has got to be the most ridiculous thing I have ever heard. How could you worry about Gary? Of course he likes you.

JOHN: I have to go pack up my things now. Bye.

What if John's father had acknowledged his feelings, and praised him for sharing them?

FATHER: I can see why you would find that upsetting. Thanks for telling me. I was worried that you were going on some kind of new crazy diet.

JOHN: No, Dad, it's not a diet.

FATHER: What happened between you and Gary?

JOHN: Nothing really. (His father waits silently.) Well, he is calling Chris a lot more now, and Rick, and he never invites me over like he used to. I saw him having lunch with both of them the other day.

FATHER: You saw all three of them having lunch. How did you feel then?

JOHN: I started to get sharp pains behind my left eyeball. I got mad and worried at the same time. And do you know what else happened with Gary?...

When John's father acknowledged his feelings and showed that he valued them, John began to talk more. This approach can often result in parents getting information they were not expecting to hear. Sometimes conversations like these are a good way to introduce the idea of Feelings Fingerprints if you have not yet done so. For John, pain behind his left eye was at least one sign of not-so-good feelings.

COPING WITH THE TRANSITION TO MIDDLE SCHOOL

One of the hardest transitions for kids to handle is starting a new school. There are so many new things to adjust to, each of which calls upon kids' decision-making and problem-solving skills. Moving from elementary school to middle or junior high school brings with it lots of issues: the school is often larger, and the child has limited time to deal with her locker and get to where she has to be next; there are older kids around—some a lot bigger—who may pick on her or tease her; there are more teachers than before, and she has to keep track of assignments and work from a lot of different classes. Whew!

Let's look in on Glenna, who is twelve and about to start Peter Guzzardi Middle School in two weeks. She will be taking a bus, and this will be new for her. Before, she went to Marcil Elementary School in her own neighborhood. Her brother is seventeen and a junior at East Central High School. Her younger sister is nine and is still at Marcil. Her parents, Walter and Darlene, are both forty-four years old. Darlene has been through this with her son Michael, but it was different because Michael was big for his age and involved in sports, so he knew older kids, was confident, and the transition was less of an issue. And, quite honestly, at that time, Walter and Darlene were not as tuned in to what was involved in the middle-school transition as they are now.

GLENNA: I have a bad headache and my stomach hurts, too.

MOM: Wow! Both at once! When did it start?

GLENNA: I don't know. It's not like I'm sick or anything.

MOM: Oh. It sounds like this is the kind of headache Daddy gets when he worries a lot, and like your brother's stomach troubles before a big game.

GLENNA: Yeah.

MOM: What might be bothering you?

GLENNA: Well, I'm sorta scared about school.

MOM: What do you mean?

GLENNA: School starts soon, and I don't think I'm going to like it.

MOM: So you're scared and maybe a little nervous because you're not sure you're going to like the new school and all the changes.

GLENNA: Yeah.

MOM: How would you like things to be better? What would you like to have happen?

GLENNA: Since I can't stay home from school forever, I guess I just don't want to be scared.

MOM: Well, what could you think about or do so that you would be less scared, and feel better about going?

GLENNA: I don't know.

MOM: Think about it for a second. You may not be the first and only person on the planet to ever go to a new school and feel this way, you know.

GLENNA: I know that, Mom! Well, like, Linda started at Guzzardi last year, I could talk to her.

MOM (nodding): Mm-hmm...

GLENNA: I could pretend I'm not really going to a new school.

MOM: You could try that...

GLENNA: Maybe I could meet someone and go together. Ellen and Patrice are going to go on the same bus, and I bet they are upset about this, too. I can call them when they get home from vacation and camp.

MOM: What do you imagine would work best for you?

GLENNA: Ignoring things never works for me.

MOM: How about your other ideas?

GLENNA: I don't like Linda that much. Maybe I'll talk to Ellen or Patrice.

MOM: When will you see them next?

GLENNA: I'll just call one of them on the phone. They'll both be home after the weekend.

MOM: Who will you try first, and when is a good time?

GLENNA: Uhh...I guess Ellen, since I like her better. But I have to wait until after eleven in the morning, because she loves to sleep!

Mom and Dad can tune into those phone calls and follow up with Glenna. They can check to see if she is reassured. If not, they can review what happened and use FIG TESPN again. They also might want to check out some books for children in Glenna's situation, such as those by Judy Blume or Mark Geller. Either way, Darlene has used FIG TESPN to get Glenna moving, open up a channel of conversation, and help her daughter avoid feeling defeated.

Let's take a quick review of how Darlene helped Glenna by using FIG TESPN, rather than by trying to solve her problems for her. By asking the facilitative questions in the worksheet, this parent helped strengthen Glenna's own social decision-making and problem-solving skills and helped her to feel confident in herself and her ability to solve problems and make choices. Darlene helped Glenna to

1. look for signs of different *feelings* (she focused in on them and use the Feelings Fingerprints that had been a part of family discussions previously);

2. state what the problem *is* ("What might be bothering you?");

3. decide on a *goal* ("How would you like things to be better? What would you like to have happen?");

4. *think* of some solutions ("Well, what could you think about or do so that you would be less scared, and feel better about going?" When Mom heard the typical, "I don't know," she used humor and broadened her daughter's perspective, to bring in others' points of view: "Think about it for a second. You may not be the first and only person on the planet to ever go to a new school and feel this way, you know.");

5. for each solution, *envision* all the things that might happen next;

6. choose the best *solution* ("What do you imagine would work best for you?");

7. *plan* it and make a final check ("Who will you try first, and when is a good time?");

8. put the plan to work and *notice* what happens, for use in solving problems and making effective decisions in the future.

ACADEMIC DIFFICULTIES IN MIDDLE SCHOOL

Harold and Cici James have a son who has academic problems. Harold works for the city's sanitation department. Cici works part-time in an optometrist's office. Their son, Franklin, is eleven and is having difficulty at school. Their younger children, Aisha, four, Linda, five, and Shawn, seven, like school and are doing okay so far. Franklin's problems are new to them. Cici's sister, Ramona, is also at the house and has an opinion.

CICI: I don't understand it. We work with him, he works. He may fail three classes. I don't know what to say.

HAROLD: Do you remember what it was like when you were in school?

RAMONA: Remember, nothing. That boy is headed for serious stuff. Just you wait until he starts going out at night, staying on the streets...

HAROLD: Ramona, that's not what we need to hear.

CICI: Well, it's possible, isn't it? If he stops caring about school, why won't he just go off with his friends?

HAROLD: All right, we are upset, we all said it in our own way. What do we want for Franklin?

CICI: Well, we want him to get back on track and do well in school.

RAMONA: He is going to ruin his life, and we are just yappin' away.

HAROLD: Do you think Franklin wants to ruin his future?

RAMONA: No, of course not, but...

HAROLD: Then let's see what is on his mind and talk to him about what is happening.

Notice that as Harold talks to Franklin, he will use modeling, suggesting, and open-ended questions to help Franklin become clear about his goal. When academic problems arise for children, it is important to clarify that there is a common goal, one of learning. The earlier such problems are addressed, and the younger the child, the easier these kinds of conversations are likely to go. But we have had them with kids from twelve to eighteen years old, and college students as well. When you stick with it, you can get to a point where FIG TESPN can help generate a plan of action.

HAROLD: Franklin, these grades are upsetting to me. But they are your grades, and I want to know how you feel about them.

FRANKLIN: I'm not surprised. I knew they were coming.

HAROLD: Now they have arrived. Are you feeling proud or upset or nervous or what?

FRANKLIN: I am nervous and upset.

HAROLD: Okay, let's think this through together. What are you nervous about?

FRANKLIN: I am nervous because I've been listening to all of you talking about me and I don't know what you're gonna do.

HAROLD: What are you upset about?

FRANKLIN: I am upset because my grades have gone down and I can't get them back up.

HAROLD: Can't? What do you mean?

FRANKLIN: I mean I have been studying and trying, but it just isn't working like it used to.

HAROLD: Well, if things could go any way you wanted them to, what would you want to have happen?

FRANKLIN: I would get good grades again. And...

HAROLD: What else?

FRANKLIN: I would make everyone proud of me again by being on a club or a team or something. I wanted to write for the school newspaper, but I may not be able to if my grades are low.

HAROLD: Well, son, this is starting to sound a little complicated. Let's get a piece of paper, write down your goals, and do some planning for ways to get those grades up and also have you join some clubs and maybe even write for the paper. We'll take them one at a time...

Where things proceed from here depends a lot on the family. Will they focus on academics? Will they support Franklin in trying to do the paper? Whatever happens, the major accomplishment here is that the family gave Franklin a chance to talk about his feelings. He was sitting with them, day after day, which made it even harder for him to do his work and learn. It is possible that although Franklin's learning styles and skills have worked up to this point, now he may need some special assistance to adjust to new kinds of academic demands. Again, the earlier this happens, the more likely it is that a child can approach the situation with hope. Without hope, the task of learning is like mountain-climbing in dress shoes—slippery and dangerous.

HOMEWORK

In some households, homework is not a large issue. But in most households it provides one of the great tests for Emotionally Intelligent Parenting. Homework usually is not especially appealing to children, especially when compared with talking on the phone, exchanging messages over the Internet, watching television, listening to music, playing sports, or, for some, breathing. It is hard to "sell" the long-term benefits of good work habits, doing homework to get better grades, learning the material better, or getting into college, especially when there is something immediate and tangibly appealing right at hand. Don't expect, by the way, that your child will rush to do homework in areas of strength any faster than in areas of weakness. In both cases, though for different reasons, your child may be avoiding homework, in the one instance through overconfidence or boredom, and in the other for lack of confidence or frustration.

Homework time will allow you to see most children's full repertoire of upset feelings. Try to help your child put the feelings into words and then try to help him or her articulate what the problem is. Once this takes place, you can start to problem-solve and plan together with many fewer emotional outbursts— by you or your child. As you will see in the examples that follow, homework is not just about doing the work; it is about being prepared to do the work, and also following through to make sure it is done properly and in a way that builds pride, rather than diminishes it.

HANDLING HOMEWORK HASSLES

A useful tool for handling homework problems is the Homework
Time chart. What this does is to help keep homework from
becoming a major parent-child battleground by turning homework hassles into problems to be solved. Although it often
doesn't seem this way, homework is more your child's issue than
it is yours. So you can take a helpful stance by working toward
resolving the problem, as Luz does with her son Ozzie:

LUZ: Ozzie, what did you write on the homework chart?

OZZIE: I was working in the kitchen and I was feeling mad
    because I want to watch the game and this reading takes so
    much time and there is so much.

LUZ: So there are two problems, yes? You will miss the game, and
    the homework is taking a long time to do.

OZZIE: *Sí.* Can I watch the game, *Mamita?*

LUZ: *Mi admoso,* first you have to get your work done. But maybe
    if you are making a lot of progress, you can watch the begin-
    ning, then finish your homework up, and watch the end.

OZZIE: But there is no way I'm going to be able to finish. Look.
    Look at all that I have to do.

LUZ: I wonder what the teacher was thinking when she assigned
    that all to you today for tomorrow. I may call her and ask her.

OZZIE: Well, I got the assignment on Monday.

LUZ: Ahh. So another problem is that when you leave big assign-
    ments for the last day, you miss out on fun things and you have
    to work much harder and longer and under pressure.

OZZIE: I guess so.

LUZ: When is the best time of day for you do to this kind of read-
    ing assignment?

OZZIE: I never really thought about it. I guess it's in the evening
    or on weekends, not in the afternoon. That's siesta time, or
    maybe time for easy stuff like math or lab write-ups.

LUZ: How are you feeling now?

OZZIE: I'm a little mad at myself. But hey, can we talk later? I have all this reading to do, and this is my best time…

The chart helps to focus on the goal, reduce tension and parental blame for homework problems, and in other ways builds important emotional intelligence skills in your children by exercising their planning skills and helping them to learn about their best and worst times to do different types of academic tasks.

HOMEWORK TIME: TELL YOURSELF WHAT THE PROBLEM IS

Example: Where were you trying to do homework? In the kitchen.
How did you feel?   Frustrated.
How could you tell?   I was slamming the pencil on the table and my face was very red.
What is the problem? I feel frustrated because I have two pages of math problems to do, and I don't know how to do them, and I want to talk to my friends on the phone tonight.

Where were you? _____
How did you feel? _____
How could you tell? _____
What is the problem? I felt _____
(when or because) _____

_____
_____

HELP CHILDREN ORGANIZE THEMSELVES
FOR THEIR BEST EFFORT

Homework also requires a certain amount of preparation. Some children are quite disorganized. Assignments are lost, things are done at the last minute, and when they finally sit down to do something, they sometimes don't have the necessary book or worksheet, and the quality of what they hand in seems pretty messy. It's natural for parents to wonder why this is and what might be done about it.

Do you remember a period of school known as "study hall"? For most students, this is a time to fool around, draw, and day-dream; only for the more organized students is it a time to get some work done. More and more educators are realizing that youngsters differ in how organized they are and that these differences may be related to overall school (and life) performance. A child who is at least somewhat organized has a better chance of keeping track of assignments, of not misplacing materials, and of having the time to turn in work that is not too sloppy—and perhaps even neat!

To both parents and teachers, it is clear that many—perhaps even most—students do not "do their best" and use their abilities to their fullest. Particularly in the middle-school years, one way to help children perform better is to help them find ways to be better organized, to listen and concentrate more, and to focus their energy so that they can get their schoolwork done efficiently and with less wasted time. Success in school, in the world of work, in sports, and in many other areas of life requires us to be able to channel our talents to get certain things done. And with so many competing demands and pressures on children, parents can help make sure their children have at least some skills at organizing themselves. Here's how:

Help create a good study environment
Where do your children do their work? Many children do their best when they have ample space free of distractions (toys, magazines, crayons, Game Boys, telephones), decent lighting, and freedom from frequent disruptions. Some children may need a quiet place. For some, disappearing in their room is a sure way to waste time. Parents need to keep tabs on what is going on, work-wise and otherwise, when kids are "studying" in their rooms.

Others do better when they work in a public space, such as a school or public library. Children do not always seek out or create study environments that are best for them. So, take an active role in helping plan, find, and maintain a work space that can "work" for your children.

Find a way to monitor assignments

This is easier said than done, but it is important to be persistent about it. The first step in being organized is for children to know what they have to do, what supplies they need to do it, and when it is due. Some system for having assignments written down and routinely shared with parents often is necessary. Some middle schools are using "agendas" that students have to complete for each class, noting the assignments they have and entering long-term assignments, but too few schools do this and take it seriously. Discipline is needed to make sure entries are made for each class, even if it is to say "No H.W." If your children continue to need reminders, you can set up telephone or Internet "check-in" times for your child to contact friends just to make sure nothing has been forgotten. Some schools post homework on voice-mail systems. But in some cases it will be necessary for you to ask the school to send home a signed daily assignment list, or confer with the school guidance counselor or school psychologist to set up a system that will work for you and your children.

Be sure work is done in order

Children often have several daily assignments and one or two long-term projects, or upcoming tests, to juggle at once. It is difficult even for us as adults to organize our responsibilities—so let's help our children develop some skills in this area. There are no easy answers here. So much depends on your family's routines, on children's after-school activities, on their bedtimes, and so forth. But this makes it even more important to help your children try to plan when to do what! Questions like these are helpful:

- What do you have to do for tomorrow?
- What do you have to do by the end of the week?
- Are any big tests coming up? When? Any reports? When will they be due?

Many families find it helpful to write this information down, and then check the daily routine and the long-range calendar. A time-planning computer program may be useful for organizing this information. The next step can be more or less direct, as your children require:

"Okay, here's what's going on. How do you plan to get things done? What will you do tonight? What will you do first?" Or, "Okay, here's what's going on. I think you'd better start with this, and then do that. Since we'll be away a lot of the weekend, you'll have to find the time to do the reading for the project during this week. How about after school on Thursday, you won't make any plans…?"

These conversations will of course vary with the ages of your children and how organized they are. But parents play a large role in managing the daily schedule, and it is helpful if this schedule recognizes the child's school responsibilities. Further complexities added by families with strong religious observances, or households in which children split time with different parents, require this type of planning even more. And when your child really does not have the time to do his or her best work, you'll know it and you can adjust both your expectations and your reactions.

Although parents may see many ways their children can become more organized, some cautions must be noted. Old habits are hard to break. Start slowly, with perhaps one or two of the approaches outlined earlier, or your own related ideas. Pick and choose, and keep trying until you find something that seems to work. Then stick with it for a while so your child can build a sense of being more organized. Next, work on adding some new aspect. It's also best to start building that sense of organization early; grades four through six are probably prime times to take a look at your child's work habits and seriously try to help out as needed. But remember when you have ever dieted, given up smoking, tried to exercise, or in other ways changed old habits—and BE PATIENT!

BE PROUD OF YOUR WORK!

Too often, schoolwork is something to be finished as soon as possible, if not sooner. If it is complete at all—which is not always the case—then there is a good chance it looks as if it were done in an attempt to win some sort of speed-writing competition. Word-processed stuff may look a little neater, but corner-cutting comes through in other ways. What's a parent to do? The time-honored answer: nag and threaten. This is sometimes effective, but labor-intensive for the parents, and not fulfilling.

Checking one's work is a habit that can be developed. Have your children show you their work, and ask them such things as "How did you check this?" "How do you know your teacher will be able to read this?" "Are you sure you answered the right questions and followed the directions? Let's see..." Sometimes creative checking helps. Arrange to have a neighbor or a nearby relative occasionally look at an assignment. Children can exchange papers with friends or siblings. Look for ways of getting out of the "police officer" role, especially if your child is careless and is not responding well to your urges to check the work. The key is helping your child feel a sense of pride in presenting a good effort, and that is often learned first by caring about the reaction of someone who will see it. Here is an alternative we like a lot. It's called the Pride Check, and it is based on a key idea that math teachers especially love: Make *checking* the work part of *doing* the work!

About an hour before a child's bedtime, children show to Mom or Dad the work that is going to go to school the next day. It is going to be looked over for neatness and completeness. Make the point that we should be proud of our effort and that we need to make it clear that we worked on the assignment and care about the teacher who is going to have to look at it. It's a matter of respect. This is not a check of accuracy, necessarily, so it's something parents can do even if they do not feel completely confident about the content of what their children are doing. But if twenty questions were supposed to be answered, they all should be done. In math, the work should be shown, checks should be visible, and erasures should be pretty clean. If there seems to be a problem, it is still early enough in the evening to catch it. Even if work is not finished, the trends of neatness are likely already established.

Variations on this include everyone bringing their work at the same time and having siblings comment on each other's work, and even having parents bring work that they might have due, so they can model the process. Some families, finding this tough to do all the time, have certain nights when they do it, perhaps every Sunday or on Sundays and Wednesdays. Another option is to have your children do a little rating sheet or checklist with all or selected assignments. Some parents prefer to wait to do something like this until after there seems to be a problem. Our advice: don't wait too long. Positive work habits are hard enough to maintain. When they have to follow ingrained bad habits, the task is that much more difficult. Here are the kinds of questions that might go in a checklist:

1. I checked to see that I did every part of this assignment:
Yes _____ No _____ I couldn't because I'm not exactly sure what the assignment is. _____
2. Wherever I could, I checked my work and I showed that I checked it. I checked it and showed it _____ Checked, not shown _____ Oops _____
3. My work is neat, clear, and spelled correctly. Neat _____ Clear _____ Spell-checked _____ Proofread _____
4. On a scale of one to five, this is how proud I am of the work I am handing in:

1 = really proud
2 = kind of proud
3 = a little proud
4 = not proud
5 = ashamed

BALANCING HOMEWORK AND CHORES
IN THE DAILY ROUTINE

DAD: Phil, it's 7:00 P.M. and you have a lot to do tonight. What's your plan?

PHIL: I don't know. I guess I'll do my homework.

DAD: Good idea! What do you have for tomorrow?

PHIL: Uhh, math, science, reading.

DAD: Wow! How much of each?

PHIL: I don't know.

DAD: How about if you show it to me?

PHIL: I, uh, don't want to.

DAD: Okay, it's nice to know you don't want to. But you have to because I need to know what you are doing in school. It's a dad thing. When you were born, I had to sign papers saying that I could be quizzed at any moment about how you were doing in school. They never said what the penalty is for not knowing, but I don't want to take the chance.

PHIL: Dad, get real.

DAD: Phil, get your backpack.

Once they take a look at the homework, Dad knows the time is right to remind Phil that homework is not his only responsibility:

DAD: Are there any house chores you need to do tonight?

PHIL: I don't know.

DAD: It's Tuesday.

PHIL: Oh. I, uh, have to take care of the garbage. And I want to watch something on TV at ten.

DAD: You know you can't watch until your work is done.

PHIL: But, Dad, it will take me until ten to do my homework. Can't someone else do the garbage?

Dad has lots of options now. Already, Phil is planning on doing homework from sevenish until ten o'clock—a major accomplishment. Dad can suggest Phil tape the program (but then he can't start watching until eleven, which is too late, so he would have to wait until another day), or he can suggest that Phil miss the beginning and take care of the garbage (which is a problem because the show is a mystery and the beginning is important), or he can model a possible solution and let Phil make the choice. Dad opts for the latter, and models self-prodding by thinking aloud, in the following example:

"It's recycling day tomorrow, the second Wednesday of the month. I do not like to do this—what a pain! But if I wait until next time, we won't be able to store everything, no way. There's a good program on that I want to watch. These commercials are about two minutes. If I use the next few commercials, let's see how much I can get done. First I'll get the newspapers wrapped up. I can even do that while I watch. So, during the commercials, I'll get the bottles, cans, and plastics into their containers and out to the street…"

There are lots of other occasions when we need to push ourselves, and it is useful for us to show our kids how we reason our way into action—or inaction. Especially useful is to share with kids how we can do what we are doing, or we can try to reach a better goal:

"I can sit here and read, *but* I am going to call the restaurant and make that reservation because I think we will all enjoy going there."

"I can watch television, *but* there is a new movie I hear is really good and I want to go see it, so I am going to go look up the times and plan on going."

"I can sleep late, *but* the garage needs to be cleaned out, and if I do it, we can put up the new basketball net and inflate all the balls and we can all get out and shoot some hoops in style!"

Afterwards, it's good to review what you did, and give yourself and your child some feedback on how the plan went:

"Well, I got the recycling done. I missed a few minutes of the program, which was no big deal. But I bet if I had started at the first set of commercials, I wouldn't have missed a thing! Next time, that's what I'll try."

"No reservations available until the beginning of next month! Well, I made it and it will be fun, but if I had gotten up from reading a few days earlier, we probably would have gotten earlier reservations. I won't let myself be lazy that way next time."

"Oh, do I ache. But wasn't that a great basketball game? It never would have happened if I hadn't cleaned out the garage. What a mess! I should remember not to let it get so out of hand. We actually had to throw away one of the basketballs because it got deflated and crushed under some chairs and the valve was bent. Thanks for helping me put up the net, by the way..."

ENCOURAGE EXPRESSION OF PLANS TO REACH GOALS

When your kids have said that they are going to do something, or when you have invoked FIG TESPN to make a plan, there still are next steps. After all, some children are more reluctant than others to put their ideas into action. And most kids, like most adults, do not like to be pushed too strongly. So, we encourage you to use gentle prodding. You may be doing some of this already:

Remind your child about the goal:

- What was it you wanted?
- What is it you're trying to do?
- What will happen if your plan works?

Be encouraging and confident and upbeat:

- I can't wait to hear how it turns out!
- I have confidence that you can carry it out.
- Maybe tomorrow will be a better time.

Get out any fears by helping to think about consequences:

- What do you think might go wrong?
- What if _____ does go wrong? What will happen?
- What's the worst thing that can happen? What's the best?

Sometimes gentle prodding leads a child to express hesitation or uncertainty. When this happens, a role-play practice is often a good idea. Listen:

MOM: Juan, you are still here!

JUAN: Yes, it's not time to leave yet.

MOM: Oh. What is it you are going to do tonight?

JUAN: I was going to go over to Marianna's house and see if she wanted to hang out.

MOM: Sounds like fun. I can't wait to hear how it turns out!

JUAN: Ah, well, I don't know.

MOM: What do you mean? What could possibly go wrong?

JUAN: She may, you know, think I'm a jerk.

MOM: I see. What is it you are planning to say to her when you first go over?

JUAN: I, ah, um, I will, ah, I'm gonna say, uh, 'Yo, Marianna, what's up?'

MOM: Well, that's one way to start. But it might be a good idea to practice a little, since you don't sound too confident to me...

Be ready to give constructive suggestions while also being encouraging. Use humor, and if your child knows Keep Calm, this is a great time to use it! It may even be useful to switch roles.

When Juan comes back, Mom follows up and helps Juan prepare for next time:

JUAN: The worst night of my life!

MOM: What happened?

JUAN: She said she didn't want to see me on Saturday.

MOM: You asked to see her on Saturday?

JUAN: Yeah.

MOM: How were things going before you asked?

JUAN: Pretty good.

MOM: So what happened when you asked her?

JUAN: She said she couldn't, she was busy with her family.

MOM: Did it occur to you that she might be busy with her family?

JUAN: Well, now that you say so, yeah. But then, I figured she just didn't want to.

MOM: Well, based on what you think now, what do you want to have happen?

JUAN: I want to see her Saturday.

MOM: Is that really the only thing you want—Saturday only?

JUAN: No, I want to see her again.

MOM: How can you try to do that?

Now Juan is back on track, and FIG TESPN is ready to roll, to help him generate ideas, think them through, and make a new plan.

A "LACK OF PROGRESS" REPORT IN HIGH SCHOOL

The mail has arrived. Your ninth-grader has gotten a progress report for the second marking period. The trouble is, this report is a "no progress" report, and you are annoyed. You had no idea that there was any problem! You'd asked your child how things were, and he'd told you, "Fine." Even when you probed a bit, there seemed to be nothing going poorly. The child is Aron, the parents are Mr. and Mrs. Pratt.

MRS. PRATT (waiting until after dinner, since this tends to be everyone's most patient time in the evening): Aron, we got something in the mail today from the school.

ARON: Oh, it's that stupid progress report. That Nagle, what a bagel.

MR. PRATT: I would like to hear a little more about that. The report said that you are failing soccer in gym, and you are also headed for a C in world history.

ARON: Really? I didn't know about the history. The soccer, well, Nagle wants us to do these strange warm-ups and to sing out loud or whatever as we do the drills. I just think it's stupid and I won't do it.

MRS. PRATT: Don't you realize how disrespect—

MR. PRATT (interrupting): Do you mind if we hear about the history so we can get the whole picture? Thanks.

ARON: There was a big test and I got a 70. I didn't think that was so bad, although most of my friends did better. But those questions were tricky. I liked it better when we had the essays. Those I understand! All these multiple choice and fill-ins make my brain hurt.

MRS. PRATT: I had a lot of trouble with those kinds of tests in high school also. But let me tell you, you'll see a lot more of them in the future. Would you like some help in figuring out how to deal with those kinds of questions?

ARON: Well, maybe. The rest of the marking period grade is going to be a group project about Peru, and I love those things. I get to make everybody else work and organize and we will have the best group project of all!

MR. PRATT: That sounds fine. Let's get back to soccer.

ARON: I can't stand it. I won't do it.

MR. PRATT: That is one choice you have. Have you thought through what will happen if you keep up what you have been doing?

ARON: No, not exactly…

MR. PRATT: What grade would you like to get in gym for the soccer unit? Picture what you would like to see on your report card. When you apply for college—and maybe for sports scholarships—what would you like it to say?

ARON: I want an A. I'm terrific at soccer.

MR. PRATT: What grade do you think you will get if you don't follow the teacher's instructions?

ARON: It's so stupid…

MR. PRATT: I am not asking about that. I am asking about your grade.

ARON: I may fail. Would I have to take it over?

MR. PRATT: Probably you would. Maybe over the summer. Which wouldn't be bad, because it would save us a lot of money on summer camp. But…

ARON: What?

MR. PRATT: I was thinking that you might request to change gym teachers. What else do you think you could do to solve the problem of having gym instructions that you don't like?

From this point on, Aron is willing to engage in FIG TESPN. He has been refocused on *his* goal and the consequences of his continued actions. That's usually the best way to handle negative progress reports—work with your child to make a plan to address the issue more constructively, rather than through misbehavior, not studying, or other actions where the intent often is to spite or rebel against teachers or other adult authorities, but the result is actually quite harmful to the child in the long run.

CHOICES ABOUT COLLEGE AND CAREER

PEG: How about another piece of pizza?

MOM: Sure. Janet, I got a letter from school today about taking the college exams.

JANET: Yeah, it's all that my teachers are talking about.

MOM: So, what do you think?

Charlene Patterson, who is forty-one years old and a travel agent, is talking to her seventeen-year-old daughter, Janet, and ten-year-old Peg. Charlene is separated from her husband, with whom she has little contact and who provides only a bit of financial support. Charlene's father, who lives nearby and spends a lot of time at the Patterson house, is reading the letter while he munches on pizza.

JANET: I'm not sure.

MOM: This is a tough decision—even harder than figuring out what toppings to put on frozen yogurt or what shoes go with your prom dress!

PEG: Are you going to leave home?

JANET: I'm not sure. Every time I think about it, I get more and more confused.

MOM: If you could picture yourself doing whatever you wanted to do five years from now, what would it be? Take a minute, close your eyes, and imagine how you would look, where you would be, how you would feel. You can try it too, Peg.

Charlene was using an important method for helping our children sort out confusing possibilities. Using FIG TESPN, it's necessary to help our children decide on their goal. How else can they—and we—plan effectively and realistically? Picturing the future as clearly and sharply and in as much detail as possible is helpful for teenagers. Even if they cannot do it the first time you ask, you begin to get their minds and hearts working in a positive direction. Come back to it in a few days, and in a few more after that. Sometimes the picture is cloudy, or it has lots of mixed images. This usually is a signal that more information is needed. Writing to schools, checking out job possibilities, talking to a counselor about vocational interests all are helpful steps along the way. Let's get back to the Pattersons:

JANET: I've got a picture of me in a classroom working with children, but I also have a picture of me teaching older students.

MOM: To be any kind of a teacher, what do you need to do?

JANET: I need to go to college, that's for sure.

MOM: Anything else?

JANET: Do well, I guess.

PEG: If you are going to be my teacher, you better be smart at something.

GRANDPA: Hey, that's a good point. If you are going to be a teacher, you will have to major in something or specialize in some way. I still remember my kindergarten teacher, Mrs. Berman. She would help me hang up my coat and ask me who I was today. Every day I was somebody else—sometimes I was Mickey Mouse, sometimes I was Superman, sometimes I was the mailman—excuse me, the letter carrier—and by the middle of the year, I wanted to be Mrs. Berman.

PEG: Grandpa, you wanted to be your own teacher? Wasn't she mad?

MOM: Hold on a second. Janet, I think you came up with a good start. Let's talk about this some more—how about after we clean up?

JANET: Sounds okay to me.

FIG TESPN will still come in handy, because they have lots of planning to do, feelings to consider, and ideas to rethink along the way. What the Pattersons have is a strategy, a way of thinking about all this that is emotionally balanced, so that Janet and other members of the family, including Peg, are not overwhelmed or too upset to move ahead thoughtfully and responsibly.

College decision-making does grow more complex and costly as each day goes by. There are many points of view about college, and we will share ours. For some children there really is a "best" college to go to, one that is well matched to their interests, personalities, and living preferences, as well as values. More likely, for these children, there are a few colleges that would be virtually equivalent. Sometimes these might include the college that a parent went to, but not usually. Most often there is no obvious "best" choice, and there may be five, ten, or even twenty possibilities that would work equally well, at least on paper. If parents dig in their heels in such a matter, it can lead to great difficulty. The proof of this is the large dropout rate from college, as well as the high percentage of students who come in thinking they know exactly what career path they will follow, only to realize after one or two semesters that it is their parents' idea of a career path they have been following. When this takes place, time and money have been squandered and feelings have been bruised.

If we could travel back in time and listen to parent-child conversations that took place during the college decision-making period, it is unlikely we would have heard a lot of emotionally intelligent parenting. Of course, sometimes the children genuinely believe the path is the right one, and it is not until they actually experience it that they realize it is not. But, more often than not, there are signs of feelings in both the parents and the children that suggest forcing, and being forced. Even if the decision is made to go ahead on a particular path, it is much easier to deal with difficulty on all sides if there is acknowledgment of hesitant feelings. A parent can say, "This was right for me and I feel strongly it will be right for you, but we may find out differently." And a child can say, "I am not sure about this. I'm not opposed and I have to start somewhere and this may be okay, but it also might not work out." The result of this kind of parent-child conversation is that the channels of communication are open.

A Final Word

Education and school-related concerns are the bedrock of family life for the critical formative years we spend with our kids once they pass out of infancy and toddlerhood. These can be years of grief, tension, and contention, or of wonder, growth, and sharing.

Actually, we can count on the former being present; the challenge is to make sure these are balanced by the latter. Much of this depends on our willingness to talk with children in ways that help them exercise their own emotional intelligence skills. By so doing, we set the stage for fewer emotional hijackings, and much more understanding of family members' feelings and points of view.

Chapter 8

Reaching the Hard-to-Reach: Places to Start in This Age of Violence, AIDS, and Drugs

■   ■   ■

Parents who are in the midst of a declared or undeclared war with their children over chores and responsibilities should recognize the fact that this war cannot be won. Children have more time and energy to resist us than we have to coerce them. Even if we win a battle and succeed in enforcing our will, they may retaliate by becoming spiritless and neurotic, or rebellious and delinquent. There is only one way in which we can win: by winning the children over. This task may seem impossible: it is merely difficult, and we have the capacity to accomplish it.

In human relations, ends depend on means and outcome depends on process. Personality and character flourish only when methods of child-rearing are imbued with respect and sympathy.
  Haim Ginott, Between Parent and Child (Avon, 1969), 84–85, 243

Some children are harder to reach than others. Some kids start out as open as can be, and seem to grow distant as they get older. Others seem hard to draw in almost from the beginning. In many cases, life difficulties such as illness, loss of loved ones, divorce, job loss, and moving are upsetting in ways that some children do not recover from easily. The ideas in the previous chapters are designed to help parents reach all children. In many cases, these ideas will work even with hard-to-reach or "difficult" children. We know this through experience and research. We also know, however, that some kids may not be reached and, in some cases, need something above and beyond what we have already presented.

We have to be ready to take special steps, because it is when children do not feel a part of school, family, religious, or community life that they are most at risk for turning to violence, drugs, or the kinds of behaviors that can put them in contact with HIV and AIDS. Kids need to be involved in constructive families and communities or else they can become jealous, revengeful destroyers or they will seek out other kinds of communities where they feel valued—a function served by many gangs and cults. Who wants this for their kids?

The proper subtitle for this chapter might be "To Reach the Unreachable Star." For every child is a star in some way, and it is toward this we must reach, and not be distracted by what our children are doing that is most difficult for us as parents. Once we believe, as Larry Brendtro—an international leader in child and youth services with broad experience as a teacher, researcher, special educator, and psychologist—reminds us in his book *Reclaiming Youth At Risk: Our Hope for the Future* (National Education Service, 1990) that every child can be reclaimed, or at least deserves our great efforts to try to do so, we are ready for the parenting approaches that follow.

In this chapter we explore three age periods, and at each of them we present an important set of activities that integrate all of the skills of Emotionally Intelligent Parenting. We conclude with some ways for parents to make the tough choices they face and will face as they try to guide their children through difficult times.

Preschool, Early Elementary
   Parent-child chat time: Bedtimes
   Apologizing
   Reading

Late Elementary, Middle School
   Friendships

Middle School, High School
   Community service

All Age Periods
   The Four C's—how to help parents get their acts together and make the tough choices and decisions needed in an emotionally intelligent way.

PRESCHOOL AND EARLY ELEMENTARY SCHOOL

PARENT-CHILD CHAT TIME

There are few things more powerful for young children than a chance to talk with a parent. This is true, whether they admit it or not, so don't bother to ask them. And it is especially true for hard-to-reach children. In many cases they need to make peace with a parent before they go to bed and face a new day; sometimes they need help in making peace with a sibling with whom they have had a disagreement or an outright fight. Finally, another powerful form of parent-child chat is reading together. Four- and five-year-olds in preschool and kindergarten experience great joy and wonder at the world. But sometimes they can be hesitant, and they might not like changes and introduction of new routines. When reading does not come easily to children, falling behind or having difficulty with reading can cause a great deal of anxiety, frustration, and a lack of confidence. Therefore we share with parents some special ways to read with their children that engage them and allow them to enjoy it even when they cannot read.

THE BEDTIME CHAT:
TIME FOR REVIEW, TIME FOR APOLOGIES

When you do notice that your child is upset, there probably is no better time to follow up on it than at bedtime. This is most certainly true for kids in preschool and elementary school, and if you have started this pattern early, your kids will accept this from you through middle school and even high school, though maybe not every single time. And if you have not done it and your kids are preteens or teenagers, we still urge you to give it a try. Bedtimes are, for most children, optimal times for getting in touch with and expressing their feelings. Partly this is because they are tired and will let down their defenses a bit, and partly it is that bedtimes are reminders of warmth, cuddling, and safety. That's why teens like those late-night, two-hour, soul-searching phone calls to their friends that we parents think should have taken place a few hours earlier. But that was before we understood the principles of Emotionally Intelligent Parenting—now we know it's prime time for them to share feelings.

Here is a hypothetical bedtime chat between Isaac and his son Jacob:

ISAAC: Jacob, you don't look like yourself. You have been restless, jumpy, very quick-tempered. Such behavior, I don't see from you ever.

JACOB: Well, Dad, I know what you mean.

ISAAC: So, what are you going to do? Just be a jumper? What would be a better thing to do?

JACOB: You mean like telling you?

ISAAC: I didn't say it, you did. But now that you said it, it's not such a bad thing, is it? I'm here, so talk.

JACOB: There really isn't any problem. Really. Dad, why does my older brother get everything and I get so little?

ISAAC: Ahah! Now we see the fur from the skin. So, you're worried about what your brother gets and what you don't get. I never knew you even thought about such things. Let me tell you a little story about your grandfather Abraham...

Isaac found out important information when he used the calm situation of bedtime to talk about his son's feelings. It is unlikely that during the day, when Jacob was restless and upset, they could have had this talk. At night, when Jacob's energy levels might have been lower, Isaac learned information that could be very valuable in his parenting decisions later on. Parents just need to take a relaxed, patient approach. If concerns do not come out today, they will come out tomorrow, or the next day—or maybe they will be relieved in other ways, through everyday interactions. The best parents can do is to create opportunities for their children's concerns to come out.

Another valuable use of parent-child chats is for apologies. And we mean apologies by parents. A young child's world is turned upside down by conflicts with important adults. Bedtime is the best time to help your child get some relief. There will be many occasions when your anger gets the better of you. Maybe you raised your voice too loudly. Maybe you spanked your child, or did so too many times or too hard. Maybe you said some put-downs that you did not mean. Or perhaps you ignored your child when you should not have. Oh yes, you probably were provoked. But, as our quote from Haim Ginott says, what choices do parents really have? We are the adults. If we cannot maintain our self-control when provoked, what can we expect from our children, especially young children?

A parental apology involves a deep understanding of our child's feelings, a great deal of self-control, and good social skills, to make the apology "work." What it does for children is immense. It reassures them about their worth and their value in the world.

It lets them know that their parents care enough about them to talk to them in a serious way and admit that they made a mistake. It allows children to learn humility, a companion of empathy. Finally, it alleviates the stress of uncertainty, shame, and doubt that children feel over having provoked or, in their eyes, deservedly caused, parental over- or underreaction.

Here is an example with a four-year-old:

MOM: Allison, I came in to say good night.

ALLISON (mumbling): Good night.

MOM: I was thinking about what happened after dinner. I feel bad about when I yelled at you for not putting your dishes away. I asked you twice before and it was the third time, but that is not a reason to yell the way I did. I apologize.

ALLISON: Okay.

MOM: I love you. How about a good-night hug and kiss?

ALLISON (opens her arms): Okay. I love you too, Mommy.

Here is one with a five-year-old:

DAD: Karma, I would like to speak with you.

KARMA: Go away. I don't like you!

DAD: Karma, I will go away in a minute. I was thinking about what happened this afternoon. I feel bad about the words I used when you were trying to ride your bike. When I said you weren't trying and you would never learn, I was wrong. When I said it in an angry voice, I was wrong. I was tired from following you up and down the block and I was worried that I would not have enough energy to teach you how to ride. I was silly and I was wrong. I think you were trying and I think you can learn.

KARMA: I'm gonna ride in the street!

DAD: Well, that's something we can talk about later. On Sunday afternoon, how about if we do some more practicing?

KARMA: All right!

DAD: Good night, son.
KARMA: Good night.

Note the key parts of the formula for apologies: "I was thinking about what happened..."; "I feel _____ about _____"; "I
apologize" or "I was wrong" or "I am sorry"; a statement of confidence and/or approval; and a positive "good night." It is filled
with the best of what we know about Emotionally Intelligent Parenting, and it will work for you, too!

SIBLING CONFLICTS

It is not inevitable that siblings will have conflicts, but it sure is
likely. Of course, you would prefer it if these were only occasional, and, when they did take place, if they were not too serious and didn't last long. Sometimes this can be helped by using
the Guiding Principles we have been working with in this book.
Here is an example:

Anthony is married to Linda. They are both twenty-seven
years old, and they have two sons, Anthony Jr. and Paul, ages
eight and five respectively. Anthony Jr., like many eight-year-
olds, especially when they are older siblings, is quite possessive
about his things. His brother, like many five-year-olds, is inquis-
itive and wants to be like his older sibling. Sometimes this can be
due to jealousy, but most often it is envy based on admiration.
However, the results can be the same. It's Sunday, and the family
has just arrived home and is looking forward to a peaceful, relax-
ing day. After a few minutes, Anthony Sr. and Linda are treated
to the sounds of angry fighting.

JUNIOR: You can't have it, you brat.
PAUL: I want it, you creep. I'm not giving it back.
JUNIOR: You give it back right now or I'm gonna hit you.
PAUL: No, and you can't make me. I'll tell Mom.
JUNIOR: Give it, now!

PAUL: No! (They start pulling and tugging and shouting.)

LINDA: What is going on here?!

PAUL: He's a bully.

JUNIOR: A bully! You brat, you started—

ANTHONY: Not another word, both of you. It's Sunday. We are supposed to be a family, not a pack of—

LINDA: Junior, what happened?

JUNIOR: Paul's always bothering me, he's such a pest.

LINDA: Now, I do *not* want to hear any put-downs. Think before you speak, and answer the question I am asking. What happened?

JUNIOR: Well, I was trying to play with my baseball card collection, you know, get them set up and put them in the holder. And Paul came over and grabbed the holder away from me and wouldn't give it back.

LINDA: Paul, is that what happened?

PAUL: He called me a name.

LINDA: Did he do that before or after you took the holder?

PAUL: I don't know.

LINDA: I think it might have been after—which is not a nice thing to do, but it is a little different from just coming over to you and calling you a name. Junior, how did you feel when he took your holder?

JUNIOR: I was mad, really mad.

LINDA: There will be times when Paul will take things of yours. He has before, and he will again. You are the oldest and he looks up to you. He wants to be like you and he wants some of your attention.

ANTHONY: Your brother loves you, like I love my older brothers Richie and Al. But we fought because I wanted some of their action, you know, some of what they had and what they were doing. My dad, your grandfather, he let the fights go, but that wasn't so good for me. And it wasn't so good for us as brothers. Too much fighting when we could have done better things with our time. You know what I'm saying to you?

JUNIOR: Yes, Dad.

LINDA: So, if what you want to be able to do is to play in peace, what are some things you can do if Paul is around?

JUNIOR: Go to another room.

PAUL: No, that's not fair!

ANTHONY: Hey, let your brother finish. What else?

JUNIOR: I could play with something that maybe Paul wouldn't care about.

LINDA: Maybe. What else?

PAUL: You could play with me, too!

JUNIOR: Yeah, I could.

LINDA: Just picture for a second what would have happened if you had let Paul play also, maybe stacking some cards, organizing a team, putting them in the holder for you, something.

JUNIOR: We wouldn't have had the fight. Maybe next time.

LINDA: You have some great ideas! I don't know about you, but I'm sure hungry. Why don't you boys go ahead into the kitchen? We'll be right in...Tony, we have to remember to remind Junior to think of including Paul when we send them off to play. It's too much to expect him to remember all the time.

ANTHONY: Yeah, and we may need to make sure he's doing something that Paul can be a part of. If not, maybe we just have to say they are going to spend some time apart. It's not fair to Junior if he has to have Paul involved all the time in everything.

LINDA: I agree. I also want to think about a signal of some kind that Junior might give when he really wants to have some privacy. Now, let's go find a snack!

READING TOGETHER:
A POWERFUL PARENTING AND LEARNING TOOL

A father is reading a book to his daughter before bedtime:

DAD: "And when Geppetto brought in his fishing pole, who was on the end of it but Pinocchio and his conscience, Jiminy

Cricket." Before we keep reading, let's look at the pictures.
How do you think Geppetto is feeling?

SARICA: Happy.

DAD: What else?

SARICA: Surprised.

DAD: How can you tell?

SARICA: His eyebrows are up and his mouth is open and he's kind
of smiling.

DAD: How about Pinocchio?

SARICA: He looks happy, too. Jiminy looks tired and wet. But I bet
he's happy to be out of the water.

DAD: How would you have felt inside if you were Pinocchio?

SARICA: Smiling and happy inside because I found my daddy.

Even with a book that has no pictures, the questions can be used
in the same way. They help children learn the signs of different
feelings, to take different perspectives, and to see how certain
events can lead to certain feelings. Going beyond the words, your
children can exercise and build their emotional intelligence. This
kind of parent-child story reading is useful for fiction or nonfic-
tion, newspapers, sports magazines, biographies, or whatever else
your children are reading. You also can do this at times other than
bedtime. Also, please do not hesitate to read your children's reading assignments, whether for language arts or social studies, using
this technique. At least these very good things will happen:

- You will help your child develop more insights into what he
  or she is reading.
- You will have a better sense of how your child reads and the
  extent to which he or she absorbs material or infers beyond
  what is there, and reads actively.
- You will spend some "quality time" together that otherwise
  might have seen you and your child off doing things separately.
- You will build confidence and practice in an academic area
  that is important for your child.

LATE ELEMENTARY SCHOOL THROUGH MIDDLE SCHOOL

FRIENDSHIP: HELPING CHILDREN BUILD POSITIVE RELATIONSHIPS

"Sticks and stones may break my bones, but names will never hurt me."

This is not true. A more accurate version of this would be, "Sticks and stones may break my bones but names will *ever* hurt me." Clichés and maxims that may have made sense in their time benefit from another look before we say that they contain wisdom for the present. For children, being the object of teasing and ridicule because they are new, different, heavy, skinny, have the "wrong" color skin or physical differences, or for no reason at all, is terribly hurtful. Some children react by isolating themselves, striking back, or, perhaps worst of all, hating themselves. Every child is worthwhile, and every child deserves to be treated respectfully by peers even if they do not choose to make him or her their closest pals.

We are not saying that all teasing is bad or that kids don't need to be able take a little ribbing and criticism. This is an inevitable part of growing up. As embarrassed as we would be to tell you some of the nicknames we gave classmates when we were in junior high school, we would be lying if we said that none of this was funny stuff. (Okay, we'll tell you a few, but you'll have to figure out how they were earned: "Bone," "Rosebush," "Abdul," "Leech." The formula is that names usually were a combination of a rhyme or alliteration on the person's name, something about their physical appearance, and/or something about their behavior with peers.) But when kids are the object of teasing and isolation over a period of many weeks, or even months or years, this is a different story. Emotionally Intelligent Parenting skills all come into play when we reach out to our hurt and socially isolated or outcast children and make it easier for them to make friends.

BEFRIENDABILITY

For parents, it is sensible to want to fortify one's children in a way that makes persistent loneliness less likely to strike. But friendships are hard to plan. They come about in part because they provide something that the rest of our network of relationships does not. So, what parents *can* do is to help children be ready to wade into the social mainstream, capable of developing some positive relationships. It's a matter of helping children become more "befriendable."

Our relationships with others are the sources of our greatest rewards. In a society that is becoming more and more complex and confusing, it is important for us and for our children to be clear about friendships and not turn this source of joy, creativity, and depth into a competition-driven burden. But one cannot be "friends" with everyone. True friends are soul mates and, as such, should be cherished and nurtured. Parents can do a great service for their children and themselves by helping them to sort out their relationships, make themselves more befriendable, and put time and energy into the relationships that are most important.

HOW TO DEVELOP BEFRIENDABILITY

Look broadly. Don't allow yourself or your children to get trapped by someone else's stereotypes of what a friend should be. It's what people are like, how they treat others, and what they have to offer by way of skills and shared values and interests that count and open up new horizons for our children. We cannot be limiting in our view of friendship as a function of age, gender, or ethnic or racial stereotypes.

Expose children to opportunities. Help your children meet people other than neighbors and classmates. Joining a club (like boys' and girls' clubs, 4-H, scouts), school performance groups, or a temple or church group can lead to lifelong interests and valuable, even lasting, friendships.

Teach children to stop the turn-offs and act befriendably.
Talk to your children about the kind of friend they are to others.
Help them see that while some behaviors attract people, others
are real turn-offs. One way to do this is with a short "quiz"—
answers can be given as "always," "sometimes," or "never":

I keep the promises I make to people I know.
I let people know I like them.
I really listen when others talk to me.
I apologize when I am wrong or hurt a friend's feelings.
I go out of my way to help friends.
I return things I borrow from friends, in the same condition as
    when they were lent.
I talk over problems with my friends.
I share things with my friends.
I know what my friends like and don't like.
I brag about myself to my friends.
I say unkind things about my friends.
I embarrass my friends in front of others.

The Un-befriendability Factor is indicated by "always" or "sometimes" answers to the last three questions and not many "never"
answers to the first nine. The opposite pattern shows that a child
tends to be befriendable and, with proper opportunities and a
dose of good fortune, should establish a variety of positive, valuable, enriching relationships. Going over this list—or even having it handy when your children come home with problems with
friends—can help you and your children find friendship strong
points and some areas that need work.

HOW KIDS KEEP THEMSELVES FROM
ESTABLISHING FRIENDSHIPS

There are many reasons why children might not have friends.
Rather than discuss them all, we want to bring the most common

ones to your attention. They are not all separate. Some actually lead to others. But any one of them can stop your kids in their tracks as they try to build positive peer relationships. We will try to describe them in terms of how kids usually think about them so that parents can get a glimpse at what may be going on inside their children's heads:

"I am not like everyone else."
They are different from me, so I can't be with them. Or they won't want to be with me. Actually, I'm really a lot better than they are, so I don't want to lower myself to associate with these inferior life-forms. Or, I'm really not as good as they are. They don't know this for sure, so if I keep away from them and don't let them get to know me, they may not find out how inept, weird, alienlike, and/or just plain strange I am, and they will leave me alone.

"It's a catastrophe."
They didn't call me, so that means they didn't want me. Actually, it means they really don't like me; they probably even hate me. And so do the rest of the kids. And so do people that I am likely to meet. Or, when they teased me, I froze. I didn't know what to say. Or did I whine? I hope not! But either way, they now think I'm a real nerd, a dweeb, a loser, or even worse, a losnerweeb. This will last forever, so I'd better get used to being lonely. They will tell everyone what I did. I'm going to get teased even more tomorrow. Everyone will come over and tease me, and those who don't probably want to, but can't fight their way through the crowds of people who want to make fun of me.

"It's not my fault, it's their fault."
They are all mean and nasty. They are unfriendly. They are not nice people. Who would want to be with them? I didn't do anything wrong, it's their fault.

"I don't see why they got annoyed."

I had things to say and I said them. I don't see why they wanted to speak. And I wanted to be on line first, so I moved in front. It's no big deal, I was hungry. And they could just go get more supplies and stuff, I needed to use them and I don't like to be interrupted until I'm finished. Them? Why should I ask about them? Upset? They were upset? I didn't notice anything. They are just too sensitive.

"I don't know what to say."

I will stand there and I won't say anything, or I'll say something stupid and mundane and they will think I am weird. I am getting nervous just thinking about this. And what if they tease me? Or ask me something I don't know? Or ask me to do something that I know is wrong to do, or that I don't know how to do, or that I'm bad at? They will see or hear me and think I am the biggest idiot that ever walked on this planet. I can't handle this. I won't know anyone there, and I won't know what to say or do, where to put my hands, how to sit, how to put my feet without looking like a geek. I am not wearing designer clothes, so they will tease me for that, too. I will wait until they ask me. It may be forever, but at least I know they will want me and then they won't tease me.

"I know what to do but I just can't do it."

I'll just go up and ask how long he's been here. Or I'll ask her if anyone is sitting there, and if not, can I. Or I'll ask to get in the game, I'll ask the one who looks like he's in charge. It looks like she is the president of that club. She's the one to ask about joining. I'll ask when they meet, who else is new, who can explain things to me...But I just can't do it! As soon as I start, I freeze up, I get nervous, my heart starts pounding, my ears are ringing, I start to sweat, my hands begin to shake, I feel faint, I know I'm going to throw up or have a major anxiety attack or fall down or do all three at once.

"There's no way."
No, it won't work, won't happen, they'll never agree. Not for me, not with me, not where I am concerned. They have enough people, they are full, set, complete, no way they want me. I'm not like them, there's no way they'll say yes. Me? I don't deserve it, anyway. I was meant to be alone. It's my lot in life, my "destiny," as they say in *Star Wars*. I actually like being alone. Who needs people? I get to do what I want, when I want, how I want. I don't have to worry about anything or anyone. I can't remember when I am happier. It's the way I am, the way I was meant to be, the way my parents raised me, it can't change.

WHAT IS A PARENT TO DO?

Once these kinds of self-statements, as they are called, have had a chance to develop, they can be tough to dislodge. But there is no way for parents to tell how strong they are, so it is worth seeing if you can shake things up. Here's what you can do:

Dispute the thoughts. Say things that are counter to what you think your child is probably saying to him- or herself.

Provide counterexamples. There is a lot of false certainty in negative self-statements. Lots of evidence that their thinking is not true is right out there to be seen and heard, but it isn't. So you point out some examples. Show how kids are not all mean, how they tease a person one day, and then forget about it. Or how they pick on the kids who get nervous and don't know what to do. A lot can be gained by practicing, or role-playing, with your children so that they are forced to put their thoughts into words, show you how they will stand, what their tone of voice will be, what kind of eye contact they will show, how good they are at being their BEST. Then you can give them some specific pointers, and practice enough so that they will go out with confidence.

Some children are more likely to respond to an older sibling's, a cousin's, or a grandparent's coaching than to a parent's, or perhaps they prefer to talk to one parent about this, rather than the other. Put your ego in the pantry! Your goal is to see that your child becomes more befriendable, not to be the one to make it happen! (Many parents also find it helpful to get started with books about friendships, shyness, how to get along with others, and the like. Some kids prefer to talk first about the stories, and about the kids in the stories, instead of starting with their own situations. But eventually most will come around and bring up their own issues.)

Identify and change your children's self-statements. Talk to your children about what they say to themselves that holds them back from making friends or being comfortable in groups. If they don't seem to know, encourage them to keep track of what they say to themselves when they are in a group or other peer situations. Give them a notebook or another way to write down or record their thoughts as they have them. Then you can work to help them substitute more positive, liberating, forward-moving thoughts.

MIDDLE SCHOOL AND HIGH SCHOOL

COMMUNITY SERVICE: REACHING INTO TEENAGERS' HEARTS AND MINDS

I think I heard the word *mensch* (which applies equally to men and women) more often around my home than any other word. When I was praised for my academic excellence, I was flattered; but when I was rewarded for moral behavior and called a *mensch*, I was proud.

Rabbi Steven Rosman

Connecting with hard-to-reach adolescents is a great challenge. Usually, parents are not best equipped to do this directly. Part of this is because we are too close to the situation, too much a part of the problem, at least in the eyes of our children, to easily step back from that and put forward a solution. We are suspect. But parents can play an important role in providing access to opportunities that we know *can* make a difference. Among the most powerful of these are community service, social action, and related volunteer activity.

How does this work? It will not surprise you, we are sure, to hear that such activity integrates key emotional intelligence skills in our kids. It reaches down, below the hurt, to a child's most positive feelings and best instincts. Indeed, we often use community service activities as an indicator of how deeply hurt and distrustful and shamed a child feels. When the hurt is too great, attempts at engaging a child in these activities are unlikely to succeed. Why? The good feelings the child gets from participating in them are uncomfortable. The child's mind and heart echo with a popular movie phrase: "I am not worthy."

Indeed, that's how they feel. They do not deserve to feel good about themselves, to feel helpful, to feel that they're contributing. For most kids, these feelings will reconnect them with the best of themselves. But others, especially those who have been victimized early in their lives, may experience discomfort. In such cases they will quit the community service activity or sabotage it in such a way that they are asked to leave. Either way, we know this is a sign of deeper trouble, requiring serious and intensive professional help.

What makes community service so effective is that it involves taking the perspective of others, developing empathy, becoming aware of new (or renewed) feelings in oneself, watching what one does and says, learning how to be able to "fit" in the new environment, and the social skills to interact with others who may not be in one's usual "buddy" list. As a result of these kinds of interactions, adolescents find themselves thinking and feeling in a different way than before they began. And they feel a sense of contribution and fulfillment that they find appealing. They feel as if they are doing the "right thing." Without being able to put it into words, they feel "moral"; they feel like a *mensch*. It may give them a reason to study, to get a GED, to not get thrown out of school, even to relate to parents, or at least to some other adults, in a semi-civil way.

WHAT IS INVOLVED IN COMMUNITY SERVICE AND RELATED ACTIVITIES?

Parents have a role in providing their children with access to community service opportunities. The most likely places for this are schools, of which a growing number have community service requirements for high school graduation, religious institutions, and local communities (such as working with the poor, the elderly, homeless, young children, environmental causes, civil rights, elections). Where opportunities do not exist, or where more resources are needed, parents can help by lending their support and perhaps their leadership to efforts to provide community service opportunities to adolescents. Remember, involvement in community service tends to work better with teens, especially those who are a bit ornery or isolated, when someone other than a parent gets them started.

Should you find yourself in the role of catalyst or supporter, it will help to know what goes into an effective community service experience. It's not just a matter of showing up at a soup kitchen or shoveling snow on one's street. There needs to be a structure, one or more mentors who make sure that there is time to talk about the following "Seven R's," and make sure they are a part of your child's experience:

1. *Relationships.* Opportunities are provided to talk about the experience, to have a mentoring relationship. Also, there is a chance for talking to other teens doing similar things and for networking about future careers or education.

2. *Recognition.* Appreciation is given for leadership, contributions, effort, consistent attendance, special problem-solving or ingenuity.

3. *Respect.* There is a sense that one matters to peers, for oneself as a person and for one's efforts. Particular needs are acknowledged, such as scheduling times and locations of meetings, even translating materials, when needed.

4. *Roles.* One definitely feels needed and useful; one has definite activities and responsibilities.

5. *Rewards.* There is recognition that people will continue to do the work if they feel some sense of benefit, either in material or, as is usually the case in community service, personal terms.

6. *Results.* Accomplishments are seen to really matter; things are completed; tasks get finished; large projects are divided into smaller ones; there are visible and tangible products of the work.

7. *Relevance.* One has a feeling that one's work is part of a larger whole, a larger effort that can make a difference in people's lives.

HOW DOES ONE DECIDE WHAT OPPORTUNITY TO PURSUE?

Not every open spot is ideal for every teenager. The most successful placements result from the answers to these questions:

- What can I do? (One's talents.)
- How bad are the problems/how strong are the needs? (One's view of the situation.)
- How much can I realistically expect to contribute? (One's personal expectations.)
- How important is the situation to me? (One's values.)
- To what extent do I feel that it is my duty? (One's personal standards for involvement and action.)

To the extent to which adolescents feel they have some talents to share, see a reason to act, believe that something can be accomplished, attach importance to the situation, and feel a sense of responsibility to act, and see that friends or at least people they know or respect are doing the same thing, they are likely to move forward. Obviously they benefit from someone being able to present community service opportunities in ways that touch upon these questions, or at least make them think a bit about them. When dealing with hard-to-reach teenagers, though, that person rarely will be a parent.

HELPING CAN BE EXHILARATING, BUT ONLY IF KIDS TRY

At a time when our society is fragmented between "we" and "they" groups of all forms, it is important to note that in many cultures and traditions, giving and volunteering have often been the glue of community, affirming and advancing the connectedness of humanity.

James A. Joseph, Vice-Chairman of the Points of Light Foundation

Not too many things are more satisfying than the feelings of contribution and belonging that accompany community service activities at their best. Even most hard-to-reach teens find these feelings hard to resist. And those who are not hard to reach will derive great benefit also, enriching their growth, broadening their concerns away from the latest issue of their favorite magazines, their favorite television shows, chat rooms, or phone conversations. Children might even find themselves reconnected to the "missions" and values of their families and schools that might have seemed forever abandoned. A word of caution to parents: don't say "I told you so," don't reflect too much on how great this all is, and don't try to take any credit. These can turn kids off and lead them to quit just to prove you wrong. Pat yourself on the back in private, say prayers of thanks if you like, but don't abandon that parental scowl too soon.

ALL AGES

THE FOUR C'S:
CLARIFY, COORDINATE, CHOOSE, AND CARE

A distraught woman brought her case before the Ruling Committee of Chelm. "O Rulers," she wept, "six months ago my husband went out for a loaf of bread and never came back. What should I do?" The Ruling Committee told her to return the next day. They thought and thought. When she came back, she was greeted by the committee chairperson. "Peace unto you. My associates and I have considered every aspect of your case. Do not wait any longer. Send one of the children out for another loaf of bread."

From the legendary tales of Chelm

When parents are not on the same wavelength, even the wisest of advisers (which those of Chelm most certainly are not!) cannot always set things right. But what they will try to do is use the most basic tools of Emotionally Intelligent Parenting to help parents with their own communication and decision-making. In the previous chapters we have addressed how parents can use the principles of Emotionally Intelligent Parenting to build the EQ skills of their children and create in their homes a clear sense that EQ "matters." But how do parents make the choices they need to make when faced with their children's growth and challenging and confusing parenting situations?

Where does one begin? By now we hope you have already begun. But for many parents reading books of this kind, there are so many things to do and try, it may seem hard to know where to begin. And what should one expect? What about children of different ages? Is there something that would be best suited for trying at a particular time?

Before taking actions in their households, it is beneficial for parents to clarify their own thinking, share it with their spouses and/or other significant caregivers involved, and then decide on what action to take (or not take). This requires what we refer to as the "Four C's" of effective, emotionally intelligent parental decision-making: Clarify, Coordinate, Choose, and Care.

Why is it necessary to plan so much, to be so careful? Why not just do things by instinct, by "feel," and see what happens? There may have been times and situations in which this way of parenting worked well. And there still may be some. But in our experience, those times are few, and there are dangers now in adopting too easygoing an attitude.

Today's families come in many different shapes and sizes. There are separations, divorces, single parents, various custodial arrangements, and blended and multigenerational families. There are, in our communities and schools, epidemics of AIDS, alcohol and drug abuse, and violence. Children lacking in emotional intelligence run the risk of making choices from which they may never fully recover. The kind of "on the street" learning that was common two and three generations ago is high-risk now, because many children are walking around with churned-up emotions and a lot of confusion. They are not always thinking calmly or clearly, and are not always able to evaluate opportunities and choices that present themselves. Peer and media pressure are strong.

In light of this, parents must work to maintain the calm and reduce the stressfulness of their households; they must set up an emotionally healthy "base" and "refuge" for their children. They need places to go when decisions about violence, sexual activity, substance use, and the like become real, not hypothetical. These realities make household peace and stress reduction even more important and therefore not wise to leave to chance.

Emotional intelligence points us in the right direction by making sure that our decisions are informed by our heads *and* our hearts. Using examples drawn from real family situations in which we have worked, we provide parents with the tools they need to bring the Four C's into their homes as an aid to the process of building their children's social and emotional health.

Let's take a specific example:

Joseph, who is twelve, lives most of the time with his mother, Pam. Every other weekend and one weekday evening, he gets to be with his father, Larry. The same is true of his sister, Jennifer, who is eight. Joseph is having a hard time with his parents' divorce. He spends more time by himself and less with friends. When he does get together with friends, it is usually because they call him. But even that does not happen often, and when they do get together, Joseph does not seem to have had a great time. Jennifer seems a lot happier, more outgoing, and more involved with her friends. Schoolwork does not seem to take her very long, and she seems to have adapted well to the divorce.

Holiday time is coming. There seems to be a lot of schoolwork to finish, and a lot of shopping to do, but that depends on whom you ask. Larry believes that schoolwork needs to be done and done well always. And he feels that shopping and presents are secondary. A basic gift or two for the kids, grandparents, Mom, Dad, Aunt Mabel—those are the essentials. Gifts for teachers, cousins, friends, extra presents, and new holiday clothes all can wait. Pam feels differently. Holidays are special times. Schoolwork can be slacked off a bit. Shopping matters more right now. There are loved ones and important people who need to be remembered at this time of year. And they need to be remembered well. Also, there are religious activities that need to be attended and helped with.

Joe would be considered a hard-to-reach child, and this is good to keep in mind when facing parenting decisions. The situation we will look at is this: When Joe and Jennifer have projects to do during the pre-holiday time, they are not sure what to do. At Dad's house, it's work, work, work. At Mom's it's shop, shop, shop, or go to various holiday functions. Dad wonders why they are so far behind; Mom wonders why they have not gotten more holiday things done.

Joe and Jennifer are feeling their Feelings Fingerprints with each of their parents. They don't even want to talk about school with Mom, or shopping and holidays with Dad, because the conversation quickly becomes more stressful. In these situations, it's great if kids know Keep Calm and can use it, but this is not sufficient. Kids need these kinds of situations to be handled with Emotionally Intelligent Parenting. And here is how:

Clarify

One or both parents need to make a commitment to clarify what is happening with their kids. First, each parent must be clear. What is the issue here? What are the emotional issues involved for each child? What do I really think about presents? About schoolwork? Why do I feel that way? Is it really what I believe, or am I trying to impress someone, show someone something, make a point? What do I want my kids to learn most of all from this situation? And am I showing my confidence in them?

What might be best for Joe in another situation might not be best in this one. His emotional needs must be considered; parents cannot use formulas when it comes to their children. Joseph's schoolwork may be a safe haven for him, or it may be something he hides behind, so he does not have to deal with difficult family and peer contacts. Only knowledge of specific details will give parents the guidance they need. But parents need to be committed to seeking out the details and not rely on general rules, when it comes to reaching the hard-to-reach child.

We are quite realistic about the difficulty parents may have in doing this. It requires of parents a high EQ—they must be able to make their own feelings secondary to what is best for their children; they must be able to restrain their impulses to say and do certain things; they must be in control of their reactions so that they are not carried away, letting past events invade the present. It asks parents to have great empathy for their children's situation, and to understand their spouse's perspective. And when they must interact with their spouse—whether in person, phone, or by E-mail—to work things out, their social skills will be tested.

Yet this is the hand that life has dealt, and it is the one that must be played. Hard though it is, there are always harder hands that one can be thankful have not been dealt your way.

Coordinate

Once each parent is clear, then it is time to compare views and find common ground. If there is no common ground, parents need to ask themselves if they believe strongly that, for their children, some kind of common ground is essential. Where there is common ground, kids can feel a great deal of psychological safety. This is where they can be reached, and can thrive. For example, Pam and Larry might agree on the list of people who should get gifts from the children. This might require an evening shopping trip with Larry. They also might agree that certain of the projects due will be a priority. This means that shopping might have to be curtailed a bit so Jennifer or Joe get the necessary work time. They also might agree that Joe will need some special attention and consideration from them, maybe even to the point of involving him in some of the decision-making.

Choose

Once there is some coordination, then choices must be made: "This is what we are going to do." Parents need to take charge. There may be times when these choices can be informed by conversations with kids, and this is more true as kids get older, but there are many times when parents just have to decide and move on. This is a great favor to their children. Uncertainty, lack of clarity, and parents who do not act like parents are frustrating, anxiety-provoking, and frightening for kids. Kids' complaints about choices their parents make are tiny compared to the relief they feel at finally having some clarity and some limits. And this is especially true when they feel both parents are in agreement.

Care

After the choices are made, it's a good idea for parents to show that they care about their children's feelings. Emotionally Intelligent Parenting gives us a tool for this: keeping track of what happens. Are things going better as a result of the choices that have been made? Is there enough work time? Is the shopping getting done? Arrange check-in times just to see how things are going. If necessary, the process can start over, as the new situation is clarified and new ideas are coordinated and new choices made. We care through our attention, concern, and follow-up just as strongly as through hugs, praise, and little notes of encouragement. It is our way of saying that, as busy as we are and with all the things we are dealing with as adults, we have time and make it a priority to see how our kids are doing in important matters that a family has identified.

For a hard-to-reach child, parents need to show explicit caring and also build confidence. Parents must show the child that there is a valued role for him or her in the family, and provide assistance in areas where the child is suffering. There can be no greater parental priority.

SINGLE PARENTS, AND PARENTS ON DIFFERENT SCHEDULES

For single parents, the Four C's—Clarify, Coordinate, Choose, and Care—are useful for self-checking. Am I doing what I really want to in this situation? Have I thought through the possibilities? Have I balanced different concerns? Do I need to check with other caregivers, especially family members? For two-parent households, the four C's are just as valuable. In particular, when both parents work out of the home and schedules do not overlap in ways that allow for a lot of ongoing communication, the four C's become a form of family glue. It gives the parents a way of getting together on certain matters, and moving to a decision, a choice, rather than letting things drift.

Note that the first part of the Four C's is "Clarify," and it is something that parents do on their own. We use this because it allows the process to start without waiting for somebody else to do something or for something else to happen. When they are feeling their Feelings Fingerprints around a household issue or a conflicting point of view with another caregiver, parents need to take time, take stock, take a look at the Four C's, and take action. It's what children need and deserve.

A FINAL WORD

We began this chapter with some warnings about serious problems such as violence, drugs, and HIV/AIDS. These are most likely to strike children who have become disconnected from parents, family, school, community, and positive values. The ideas and activities in this chapter build on all others in this book, to give parents the special tools they need when they feel their children are "slipping away" from them. Different strategies are best suited to different ages. Obviously, our preferred way of working is preventive. Start when kids are young, at the earliest sign of difficulty, or even when there is *no* sign of difficulty. Parents' time is well spent in strengthening children for what lies ahead.

But no matter when parents start, there are still ways of reaching children. We do not believe it is ever "too late." As Ginott said, the work is hard, but not impossible. He was echoing sages from centuries ago, who said, "We may not finish the work, but we are not excused from starting it well." By so doing, we provide our kids with the best chances possible to succeed—no guarantees, but the best chances we, as parents in the real circumstances of our lives, can provide.

We concluded the chapter by providing the four C's. These will guide parents facing difficult decisions regarding their children, when their clarity, coordination, thoughtful choices, and caring actions can mean so much in turning around their children's lives.

Chapter 9

The Emotionally Intelligent Parenting Doctors Are In: Sound EQ Parenting Bites to Help with Common Family Issues

■   ■   ■

The following "Sound EQ Parenting Bites" are examples of brief, creative applications of Emotionally Intelligent Parenting techniques to common family problems. We have drawn them from specific questions we have been asked in workshops, lectures, and practice in schools and with families. You need not have read the book to follow these examples, but they draw on all the information, ideas, and examples we have presented.

As you consider each example, be on the lookout for how we use the principles and activities of Emotionally Intelligent Parenting. In our own thinking as these problems were posed, we kept in mind a series of questions that help bring out the five Emotionally Intelligent Parenting principles. They run through our examples and suggestions, whether you can see them or not. Here they are:

1. What are you feeling in this situation? What are your children feeling?

2. What is your understanding of what is going on? What do you think your children's understanding is? How would you feel if you were in their place?

3. What are the best ways to cope with this? What are your usual ways? How can you reduce your stress and think clearly? What are the strengths you have and how can they be helpful?

How do your kids usually cope with situations like this? What strengths do your children have that can help in the situation?

4. How have we handled things like this before? Has it been successful? What have we learned? What can we change? How can I instill confidence in the family that we can deal with this? What goals do we need to set in the short term and/or the long term? What realistically needs to happen to help us reach these goals? When will we be at our best to try to make this plan work?

5. How are we going to carry this out? What do we need to do? How will we need to approach others? Are we ready for this? Do we have the skills needed? What other ways might there be to solve this problem? If our plan hits roadblocks, what will we do? What obstacles can we think of and plan around? When can we all get together to talk about this, share ideas and feelings, and get started working on it until we are successful as a family?

If you have read the book, you will understand our suggestions in a different way. We present them as examples, but recognize that you will need to be creative in developing your own solutions to these kinds of problems, solutions that best fit your family. Every family is different, and there is no one "correct" answer to a problem. We have given you the road map and the vehicle; you still need to do the driving. It is up to you to reach your destination in a way that you find comfortable, consistent with your values, and effective for your family.

MUST HOMEWORK ALWAYS BE A BATTLE?

The problem:

Just about every day, we have struggles over our children's homework. They avoid it, they do it at the last minute, they do it carelessly—unless we really watch over them and structure their time. But it involves a lot of hassle and shouting and the like. They are now thirteen, nine, and seven. We are worried about the future, especially. What can we do about our children's homework—must it always be a battle?

This is a frequent complaint, and one of the true battlegrounds of parenthood. Many children, after a long day at school, will come home, put on the television, the computer, or a video game, and neglect to do their homework. If you are a working parent, you know the scenario: you come home after a long day of work and, just as you are about to prepare dinner, you ask your children the fifty-thousand-dollar question: "did you finish your homework?" Of course, you are not really expecting to hear that it was completed several hours ago. But you are ever hopeful! Unfortunately, it will take a little bit more than hope to have your children accomplish the formidable task of completing their homework independently. It will require you to be positive goal- and plan-oriented.

Homework should be thought of as an activity that reinforces skills worked on in school that day. Therefore, the assignment is one that children typically should be able to accomplish with relatively little intervention from you. If you are finding that this is not the case, then conversations with the relevant teachers are probably the next steps to take. However, homework is also helpful for teaching students self-discipline, independence, and time-management skills. From an Emotionally Intelligent Parenting point of view, you need to think of yourself in the role of the "consultant" and not of the "subcontractor." While your children may make great efforts to place you in the role of subcontractor, avoid this by all means. Be clear about your goal: to put a plan of action into place so that your children take more responsibility for completing their assignments.

You will find it useful to have your children complete something we call a Trouble Tracker (see pages 125–26) before you sit down and have a face-to-face conversation about homework hassles. It is a checklist/worksheet that reviews what happened, when and where, how the person thinks it was handled, what was liked and not liked about what happened, and what can be done differently next time. This is a way of taking some of the strong feelings that are involved in the situation and getting some things on paper, where you and your children can look at matters a little more calmly.

The Trouble Tracker is most useful when you and your children realize that you have some common goals. Getting homework done is in your children's interest—if not for the love of learning and scholastic accomplishment, then it can be the "ticket" to such privileges as telephone, computer, or television time.

Now the next step is to find a plan that will help everyone involved meet at least some of their needs. Using the Trouble Tracker is likely to give you some insight into the problem and give you a good starting point to come up with a plan. Rather than getting into an adversarial relationship with your children over the issue of homework, you now have the opportunity to create a problem-solving dialogue in which you and your children are more on the same "team." You also will find that the skills you have used to handle the "homework issue" will be useful in dealing with other school-related problems.

HOW DO I HELP MY CHILD DEAL WITH ANGER?

The problem:

My son is eleven years old, and lately I have noticed a lot more angry yelling around the house, and at times he will hit his sibling. With his friends, he has gotten into arguments and even fights, especially during sports. How can I help him deal with his anger?

Anger is one of the emotional states most commonly experienced by both children and adults that gets us into the most troubling of situations. It is rooted deeply in our biology, and at one time was based on "fight or flight" reactions when we felt in some way endangered. While anger may have had some life-sustaining advantage to our predecessors in their striving for survival, its very strong and frequent expression certainly has to be reevaluated in the present.

We have all experienced strong feelings of anger when we were stressed and edgy and our children began to whine or do things that irritated us and didn't respond to our requests for them to stop. As our anger builds, it is as if each annoying event acts as a mini-trigger to sustain and intensify the anger we are feeling. When feelings of anger get to a certain point, they are extremely hard to contain. This is what Dan Goleman describes, in his book *Emotional Intelligence*, as "emotional hijacking." It is what has occurred when we find ourselves doing and saying things we would never think possible when we are more relaxed and self-controlled. If this is true for adults, then we cannot be surprised that it happens to children, who have far less experience than we do in trying to successfully manage their anger.

Emotionally Intelligent Parenting provides two powerful tools to help your son with his anger. The first, called "Feelings Fingerprints," involves your son learning to recognize the earliest signals his body sends him when he is starting to feel angry. Maybe his face gets red, or hot. Some kids clench their fists, or notice that their breathing gets very heavy. There is always a signal, and the first step is to help your son keep track of those that are his. To do this, we recommend the Trouble Tracker (see pages 125–26), which can help you and your son review situations that led him to lose his cool and figure out at what point he may have started to realize what was happening.

When he does learn to notice his Feelings Fingerprints, you are ready to have him use the second tool, a strategy called Keep Calm. This involves encouraging your son to take deep breaths and count as a way of de-escalating the anger. This is quite effective, but it does take some practice to learn to do well. It's also important to catch the anger at an early point, and not when the emotional hijacking already is under way. Some children can find this hard to learn. But the Trouble Trackers will have another benefit in that they will help a child realize the kinds of situations that tend to lead him to lose his cool, so that he might try to avoid them.

The key to helping our children is to work on things when they are not experiencing anger. When we are learning new skills, it is better to practice them when the game is *not* on the line. Start with situations around the house that are not quite so anger-arousing and where you and your son both can see how he starts to "lose it." Eventually, though, it will be up to him to learn how to Keep Calm on the field of life.

Finally, what we know about Emotionally Intelligent Parenting teaches us realistic caution; anger is very strong, and it may take a while for him to bring it under control. You will help to speed up the learning process if you not only teach him new skills, but also model them so that your son will have the benefit of observing how they can be put into action.

WHEN PARENTS DISAGREE ON PARENTING

The problem:

As our kids get older, I find that my spouse and I disagree more and more on everyday parenting issues (and he is wrong, of course). It's not comfortable and I feel that our kids get caught in the middle. How can I handle it?

Contrary to what you might initially think, this may actually be an Emotionally Intelligent Parenting strength, not a weakness. Having different perspectives on a problem can make it more likely that parents will find an effective solution. A problem does occur, however, when parents do not communicate well together. What often happens then is that each parent gets more extreme in their parenting, attempting to compensate for the style (read "error") of the other. One parent is seen as too harsh, and therefore the other becomes more lenient. This parent is seen as too lenient, therefore the other parent becomes more harsh. As this cycle continues, parents get farther and farther apart and more and more extreme until neither parent is really parenting the way they want, and the marriage becomes affected as well.

The solution here is to communicate. You will need

- time to talk
- ways to talk with each other supportively
- a strategy for looking at the problem
- a motto (one we like is "to parent and to love is to accommodate")

Talk time. Parents need time and space to talk to each other. In our work with families, often all we do is provide the environment for parents to communicate with each other. Here is a BIG SECRET: If parents sat down together at least once a week to formally discuss parenting issues for an hour, many psychotherapists would be out of business. We do not have to tell you that parenting is a big commitment of time, energy, and money. You cannot short-change parenting time or it ends up costing you much more in some other ways, such as stress, unhappy children, therapist bills, or divorce.

Talk supportively. When you do sit down with your spouse or significant other, use the following as guiding principles (see chapter 3). Ask open-ended questions, where you genuinely listen to what the other person has to say. Do not make assumptions or accusations. After one person has spoken, the other should paraphrase back to check for understanding. Also, please be patient. This kind of communicating takes time, and you may not be used to it.

A problem-solving strategy. As you talk, it will help to have a strategy. We recommend FIG TESPN, which is really an acronym for an eight-step problem-solving framework (see chapter 6). It involves asking these questions: How are you feeling about your child's behavior? How do others feel about it (siblings, teachers, etc.)? What is the problem? How would you put it clearly into words? What is your goal for your child? (You will be surprised that both you and that pigheaded spouse of yours have very similar goals. That's right, he/she really does not want your child to grow up to be an inconsiderate, maladjusted failure.) Given these feelings and goals, what can you do? What else can you do? Who else might you need to talk to? And what might happen if you try these various ideas? What has happened before? Okay, what seems like it might work best to get you to your goals?

Accommodation is like stainless steel. Stainless steel, like many metals, is an alloy, a combination of two or more sometimes very different substances. The result is stronger than any one of the components. Emotionally Intelligent Parenting is similar. If you cannot reach consensus on an idea, experiment, try one approach, see what happens, and then try another if necessary. Plan who is going to do what. Anticipate obstacles and plan around them. At your next parent time, review how things are going and revise your approach as necessary. Look to find creative combinations that accommodate both parents' points of view, although not necessarily equally every time. Try to be tolerant and accepting of each other's views. Respect your spouse's opinions. Be open to combination. Continuing in your old path of parenting extremes will definitely not work.

CAR RIDES ARE DRIVING ME CRAZY!

The problem:

> We get in the car for any kind of visiting, and you would think that someone took away our generally good children and put in some kind of monsters. It is as if civilization has

been forgotten. The impatience, the shouting, the shoving, the language! Which music, who is touching whom...Help!

Nothing breeds problems better than confined spaces, boredom, and parental preoccupation. Minivans were invented by a parent who needed to separate his children during a car ride. Sometimes we suspect that fathers in midlife crisis buy sports cars because there is no backseat for children.

If you must ride with children—and it is almost unavoidable if you are a parent—be emotionally intelligent. You must be realistic about your feelings, clear in your goals, and sharp in your plans. Think about when you leave. For long trips, start at night or early in the morning so they might fall asleep. Try to plan around heavy traffic, even if it means telling people that arriving a little later or earlier will work better for you.

As for the ride itself, bring lots of toys to distract them (this is the only justifiable use of hand-held video games, and we also include Walkman-type things in this list). Laptop desks will enable them to draw and write and also set up nice "boundary" zones. There are now about 4 million more car games than when we were growing up—then, it was just the license-plate game and geography and maybe, somehow, cards. Now, there seems to be a car version of everything. Don't forget they are kids, by the way. Stamina is not their great strength. For their sake (and yours, indirectly), break up long trips with reasonably frequent stops.

Don't pretend this is all new. Prepare your children. Think aloud about what you remember from a similar previous trip. Share your feelings. Brainstorm with them about ideas for avoiding the problem. During the trip, you can remind children that "stuff happens"; the more they fight, the more distracted you are, and the longer the ride. When things get unsafe, don't hesitate to pull over to the side of the road so they can Chill Out (see page 100) or do some better problem-solving. Don't start disciplining by turning around when you are driving! You can also set up a simple chart for the ride. For every ten minutes of peace, they earn a point. The points may mean a treat at a next stop, a chance to control the music selection for a period of time, a choice of game, some extra privilege at home as a reward for their maturity and self-control, and so on.

HOW CAN BEDTIMES REALLY BE BEDTIMES?

The problem:

My husband and I disagree on how to get our children to sleep—actually, to stay in bed. One is two and the other is five, and after they get to bed they almost always climb out and visit us. I work a few nights each week, and my husband doesn't see the visiting as a big problem. But I do, especially when they are exhausted in the morning!

It's not uncommon for children to have the kind of sleep problems you describe. Usually, a child of two or three sees sleep as a separation from parents, and they wander because of anxiety. In children between four and six, the problem is more often a specific fear of the dark, of shadows, of robbers, or just of being alone. And of course, some just prefer the warmth, comfort, and security of being next to Mommy and/or Daddy. Given this, why should your children be so eager to stay in their beds?

Emotionally Intelligent Parenting gives you some tools to handle this situation. You are going to want to show your children empathy, try to understand their feelings and why they feel that way, keep track of when the problem takes place, and then, with great optimism, take steps to reassure your children that they are okay, give them the tools to check, and—here's the toughest part—stick to your plan!

First of all, talk to your kids about why they get out of their rooms. Ask if there is something that they are afraid of, or if they are scared or worried. Your older child might be able to tell you about what we call a "Feelings Fingerprint," which is a place in our bodies that signals us when we are stressed or upset. For example, when you or your husband leave the room, your child may feel flushed and red, or all jumpy inside, or feel a strong heartbeat, or something like that. Ask your children what might make them feel better while staying in bed. For a lot of younger children, doing a thorough check of the room, leaving a light on, and/or having a flashlight available is a major help.

Also important is to keep track of when and where the problems happen. Make a chart that tells you, for each child, what time the bedtime is, which parent is home, when the calling starts or appearances begin, and what happens after. A lot of the time, parents send mixed messages to kids. We know of parents who are home alone at night, don't spend a lot of time with their kids, and actually are glad when their little explorers find their way out of bed and to them. We also know that the patterns of when a parenting problem takes place give us many clues about why it occurs.

Parents need to agree on what bedtime is and what it means, often because in the morning, a tired kid is very hard to deal with. If parents want to spend extra time with a child, it's fairer and clearer to just extend the bedtime, rather than hope for or even encourage Houdini-like escapes from their bedrooms. So, if you both are clear that your goal is to have your children stay in bed, here are some steps you can take:

Make sure good-night is good-bye for the night. Tell your children, after your bedtime routine, that you will see them in the morning and that they will have to spend the night in their cribs/beds and nowhere else. This is the last chance for kisses, hugs, stories, checking for aliens, or anything to drink (not a great idea for other reasons). If there is a genuine bathroom trip needed, decide if the child can just go and take care of it or if calling you is okay. If a child wanders after that, immediately bring the child back to the bed with very little conversation (also with no particular anger or joy—as if you were returning a book to a bookshelf).

Set up a chart for keeping to the sleeping routine. On your refrigerator, let your children put a sticker in a box for a night without journeys. If you want, when there are a certain number of stickers in the week (you can start with four and gradually work it up to seven depending on how often the problem takes place), your child might earn a treat, an extra bedtime story, a bedtime fifteen minutes later on a given day, or a small puzzle or book. But most kids just love the charting and will even respond to "working" for bigger and better stickers! Gradually, you will find you can phase out the charts—but don't rush to do this too soon. Wait at least a few months.

When kids resist, be understanding but firm. When some children find they are not going to be able to stay up, they don't come out again, but they do start to cry. Loudly. Our advice is that you need to stick it out. Try to wait fifteen to twenty minutes before going in. This seems like forever, but most kids will stop crying and fall asleep before that, and if they cry again the next night, they will do it for a shorter time. The next morning, make a point of saying that you are here, their room is here, all is safe— just as you said it would be. Your reassurance is powerful, but it still may take a week for this to work. When you hear a child in truly great distress—and some kids are great at this—you might have to go in, but don't take your child out. Be brief—wipe off tears, blow noses, and then say, "You are big enough to stay in bed. Mommy (and/or Daddy) is here, and we will be here in the morning. I'll tell you what—as soon as you're asleep, I will come in and check on you." And then say good night and leave. You'd be amazed at how many preschoolers and young children feel reassured by this approach. For the more suspicious, you may make a deal and tell them that you will leave something in their room when you come in so that they know you checked on them. This could be a tissue, a special sock, or something else soft and safe.

Remember, tonight's sleep problem is tomorrow morning's misery. Be consistent, and you will reach your goal.

DEALING WITH TEEN DISHONESTY,
LYING, AND CHEATING

The problem:

> My teenage son, seventeen years old and a junior in high school, lies to me all the time. He cheats on his schoolwork, and in general he is dishonest with teachers and even with his boss in his after-school job. I don't know how things got to this point. What can I do?

Parents want to be able to trust their children. There are few things more important than that. When the trust seems not to be there, it can be an awful feeling. But remember—this is true for your son also. He does not feel great about lying. But, like most habits—and lying and dishonesty often become just that, over time—it is hard to give up.

Now, let's make a couple of assumptions. Let's assume your son knows right from wrong and usually realizes he is lying. We don't need to teach the kind of basic lessons we would with a younger child. Emotionally Intelligent Parenting usually begins with asking, "What is the problem from my child's point of view? How is my child feeling?" and "When does it seem to happen and not happen? What are the patterns?"

When teenagers lie, it's usually because they don't want their parents to know that they are doing something the parents would disapprove of, because they are insecure and are using the lie to get something that they don't feel they can earn through their own talents, and/or to avoid a situation where they will feel great failure or discomfort. The teen years are times of experimentation much more than they are times of rebellion. So, teenagers since the earliest pimple have needed to keep some secrets from their parents. They know their parents have a certain image of them, and they may not want to tarnish it. It is most unlikely that you were much different when you were a teenager.

However, lies in this situation are not the same as lies related to homework, work responsibilities, household chores, and the like. There are lots of ways to get tough in the face of such lies, to make sure there are consequences and that they are followed through completely. But before trying such things, we feel that there is a larger issue at stake: your relationship with your child. What will it be? We have seen patterns of lying and parental punishments lead too many kids away from their parents and into the waiting arms of gangs and other antisocial peer groups.

Reflect for a moment on what our oldest advice is about parent-child relationships: children must honor their father and mother. Please note that the word is not "obey," and some feel that a better translation of "honor" is "respect." Respect is a mutual relationship, something that gets received more strongly by giving it more strongly. Obedience, especially out of fear, is likely to bring resentment and rebellion, often in the form of dishonesty.

How do we gain our teenagers' respect? We do this by showing how we care for them and value them—by finding and praising their strengths. We do this by seeking out their opinions and valuing them—making them a part of our lives, of the everyday life of the house, and therefore partly responsible for decision-making that usually affects them, also. And we do this by showing tolerance for misbehavior that is the inevitable result of growing up and experimenting to find one's own way. We must keep the channels of communication to our teenagers open, although we may have to experiment a bit and find out the frequency that will allow the communication to get through! So we need to keep track of when our relationship with our child is best. When are things honest? When do our best conversations occur? What are the "safe" areas and the best times of day or night? Some parents find that the best way to communicate what will be perceived as nagging reminders when given in person is through E-mail or phone machine messages to their teens. Sadly, there are times when things between parent and teenager have gone so far that one can find little to build upon. In such cases, we suggest that you look harder, seek out smaller positive moments, and also look to your teenager's relationships with other family members. Sometimes that gives parents a way to restore a communication channel.

Wipe the slate clean. However difficult this may seem, we find that most of the time the best thing for parents to do is to sit down with their dishonest teens and declare an amnesty. What happened in the past is in the past; we need to build a relationship together for our future. This requires, at times, serious soul-searching by parents about their own honesty. Kids pick up on things—business relationships; tax stuff; phone conversations in which your words and facial expressions are at variance with each other; how parents treat family, friends, employers, and neighbors. We need to engage in mutual respect, which begins with honesty. And parents will need to make the first move most of the time. Explain to your son that you have confidence in him. Point out his strengths. Be sure your expectations for grades, athletics, and work accomplishments are realistic. Disappointment occurs when the impossible is believed to be expected and, of course, it is not achieved. Set up some realistic goals and standards and talk about working together. Open up the channels, but make it clear also that you cannot protect your son from the consequences of his dishonesty. You are there for him, but the law is the law, school rules are school rules, and people often treat others as they feel they have been treated.

Above all, don't expect that your child will change immediately. This is a gradual process because, like any habit, dishonesty can become almost reflexive and therefore hard to stop completely and quickly. He needs to check you out, to see if you will keep your word and focus more on his strengths and be understanding about his difficulties. Respect elicits respect, and honesty will come along for the ride.

Setting Limits with Teenagers

The problem:

My daughter is fifteen, and her friends seem to be able to stay out as late as they like, use the phone as much as they want, get on-line on the computer without restriction, see R-rated videos and movies, and shop as often as I do laundry—which is often. I am not aware of many of them continuing their religious instruction or attendance, or of their having real responsibilities at home. Am I old-fashioned? I don't think this is right for my daughter, or for my younger sons.

Old-fashioned? No way—you are on target for twenty-first–century parenting! You seem to know the answer already—the parents of the teenagers you describe are not doing them any favors. But how do limits get set? Which ones should we stick to? How do we decide? These are the most difficult questions you are asking.

If we want our teenagers to grow up to be self-disciplined, responsible, and thoughtful, we must give them opportunities to make choices and deal with limits. And we need to start early, no later than your daughter's age, because there are lots of tough issues ahead, such as cars, dating, drinking, parties—some of which you may be dealing with now, but will only get more serious as kids grow older.

One of the main reasons we find that parents have difficulty setting limits is that they do not have clear goals for their families, or for their children. When one looks at an opportunity to go out, to talk on the phone, to be on the computer, it is not hard to look at each one and say, "What's the big deal?" The big deal is, where does it all lead? What is it doing for our family? For this child? Is the money we are spending being spent wisely, or do we have certain goals that we need to be thinking about when we spend money? Do we want our kids to be well read, in addition to being well videoed? Do we care when our kids get exposed to the kinds of violence, language, and sexuality that earn movies their R ratings?

Parents need to take stock of what goals they have for themselves and their kids. Certain things will contribute to those goals and certain things will not. Some things can and should be what Yakov Hilsenrath refers to as nonnegotiable. These are areas in which you have the strongest values and feelings and will not change your mind. Of course, as children enter significant new age periods, these things need to come up for review and discussion—like seeing R-rated movies once they turn seventeen or eighteen. But that doesn't mean you are going to change your mind.

Nonnegotiability extends beyond the "thou shalt nots" of family life. You may feel you want your child to continue religious instruction, do some kind of volunteer or charity activity, take responsibility for certain specific things as part of the home routine, keep in touch with certain relatives, or do other things that are important to you. You may make it clear that these will have to be done before other things—like phone use and shopping. You have every right to teach your child responsibility, and this is a major way of doing so.

A few points of warning. The earlier you start with kids, the easier it is for them to understand the logic of what you are doing and to eventually accept it. Don't get into the trap of expecting gleeful compliance. What is most important at first is compliance; the glee may or may not follow. Be sure to bring up your ideas and values for discussion, at least twice a year. Listen to what your kids have to say when they ask you to modify your position. Question their reasons and listen carefully. You may find yourself modifying some things. When this is done in a reasoned discussion, it usually is a positive thing. But make your changes gradual. And don't be afraid to bring back an old limit if you feel it is necessary. Just remember not to let your children feel that a limit, once changed, is changed forever.

Goals, communication, and nonnegotiability—essential tools for Emotionally Intelligent Parenting!

WHAT DO I DO WHEN MY CHILD IS VERY SAD?

The problem:

I read so much about depression in children lately, and I am confused. At times, my child looks very sad. Is it serious? How should I handle it? What is the best way to approach my child when this happens?

It is not unusual for children to feel sad about things as they are growing up. Some children are especially sensitive to their surroundings and tend to internalize feelings rather than act them out. Many children may experience sadness as a result of a perceived or real loss. It is not unusual for children to experience sadness as a result of difficulties or conflicts that have occurred with their peers. This often happens in school as children begin to define themselves and change the groups that they are associating with. While brief periods of sadness are to be expected during childhood, it is important to monitor children carefully to ensure that they are not experiencing clinical depression.

Sadness is one of the basic human emotions that all children will experience at one time or another. When it surfaces initially, emotionally intelligent parents go to the "toolbox" and pick the right tools to address the problem. First, it will be important to open up communication with your children and reflect back to them how they are feeling. When you ask about feelings, you will need to ask follow-up questions, what we call the Two-Question Rule (see page 73). Begin by asking the child how he or she is feeling. Then be prepared to follow up by saying, "How are you really feeling?" or "I noticed how you looked when you came home from school, back from friends, etc. How were you feeling then?" Remember to stay in the questioning mode so that you can begin to gain insight into the problem they are experiencing.

There is a good chance that your child is feeling sad because of some perceived loss—of friends, status, security, or self-esteem. Your job, through your facilitative questioning and reflecting back to your child what you hear, is to listen and let your child know that you empathize with how he or she is feeling. Try to take your child's perspective and imagine how the world looks to him or her. There are times when just understanding your child's sadness will be an important source of relief.

If you have a child below the age of five who is feeling sad, then you can sit down with some paper, pencil, and crayons and encourage expression of feelings through drawings. Drawing is a wonderful activity for children who are feeling sad and need an outlet for their feelings, and it provides a visible barometer of what is happening to them internally. As a child starts to feel better, this will probably be reflected in the drawings. Also, let your child pick out books to read. You will see the titles changing as the mood gets sunnier.

As the parent you will have to judge how best to approach your child and help to work through the sadness. Sadness is common among children and has an adaptive component that may not need to be worked through. If this is the case, then just validating your child's feeling may be all that is needed. However, if you feel your child is stuck in this emotional state, you may need to work to change your child's perspective on what is happening. Research in the field of emotional intelligence suggests that one of the best ways to deal with sadness is through the use of distractions. Distractions tend to break the urge to ruminate on the negative thoughts that may be associated with feeling sad.

With this information, you can try to help guide your child into another mind-set. Some of the best activities are physical, such as aerobics, sports, exercise, even dancing. For older children, volunteering and community work are effective mood-changers. And those old standards, uplifting TV, movies, video games, and puzzles, can engage children enough to shake the sadness.

Keep in mind that these tools of Emotionally Intelligent Parenting are addressing the kind of sadness that is a part of everyday life. When they do not work, when the sadness lingers and interferes with eating, sleeping, socializing, and schoolwork over a period of a few weeks, don't hesitate to contact your school's guidance counselor or psychologist, or another mental-health professional.

HOW DO I GET EVERYONE OUT OF THE HOUSE IN THE MORNING, INCLUDING ME?

The problem:

I am a smart person. I work, I volunteer, I do a lot of hard things. But I cannot get everyone out of the house in the morning without wearing myself out, or feeling as if I am going to strangle someone or just run out the door and never come back. I try to rush them along, and they move in slow motion. Why can't I handle this better?

Psychologists have discovered something that Einstein did not. $S = 1/PT$, and $PRW = 1/S$. This means that the speed of children's movement (S) is inversely related to the time in which the parent has (PT). In other words, the less time you have, the longer the child takes. Interestingly, Parental Rushing Words (PRW), such as "hurry up," also are inversely related to the speed of the child, therefore slowing the child further. A related finding is that the greater the importance for the parent to be on time $(IPBOT)$, the less likely it is that the child will be ready, or $S = 1/IPBOT$. Combined, $S = 1/PT - 1/PRW - 1/IPBOT$. Simplified, Morning Stress and Rush equal Trouble and Slowdown!

Though many have speculated on the reasons for this "rush slowly" phenomenon, we believe it is related to stress. Very, very few of us function well in times of high stress, whether parent or child. A common reaction to stress is to slow down to deal with whatever is happening. Therefore, the more stressed the parent is about leaving, the slower the child moves, the more stressed the parent becomes, the slower the child moves, the more stressed...

Step back from your morning routine and ask what the problem is. Often it is that there isn't enough time to get ready. Bite the bullet and readjust schedules as necessary. "Yeah, easy for you to say," you say? Emotionally Intelligent Parenting is about being realistic and certainly about being aware of our feelings. Think preventively. If getting the kids in bed a half hour earlier and up a half hour earlier can save mornings of yelling, heartache, and being late, isn't it worth it? And if they don't like it, all they have to do to get the old routine back is to be on time in the morning with minimal hassles. Life is always a matter of choices and consequences. Problem-solve with your kids, but set a clear goal. Make your decisions consciously rather than just letting things happen. See what other schedule adjustments can be made to free up more time in the morning.

Time is not the only issue, of course. You also need to use some Emotionally Intelligent Parenting strategies for managing the wasting of available time (see chapter 4). Praise everyone for behavior that is consistent with getting ready. Point out that "stuff happens," such as they may miss breakfast, have to pay for your gas if you have to drive them (again), or will get detention if they are late to school. One mom told her son that she was leaving the house at 10 minutes to 8 in the morning and so was he, dressed or not. It took just one time of her taking his clothes in a bag and putting him in the car in his PJs before he shaped up. Set up a chart to delineate the sequence of steps for getting ready and monitor the child's performance (get up on time, wash, dress, make bed, eat breakfast, etc.). Occasionally, take special requests for breakfast foods or cooking as an incentive, even if the latter has to wait until a weekend.

With adolescents, we recommend that you make them responsible for working through the problem, using FIG TESPN (see chapter 6). In this acronym, *F* is for stating Feelings; *I* is for Identifying the problem; *G* is for stating a clear, positive Goal; *T* is for Thinking about different ways to reach the goal; *E* is for Evaluating how well each will do; *S* is Selecting one that seems best; *P* is for Planning how to make it work in the real world, including anticipating pitfalls; and *N* is for saying, "Now what—how did it work, what might we do next time?"

For example, the adolescent may respond:

F = I'm tired, angry about going to school.
I = I'm not a morning person.
G = I want to graduate from high school.

T = Put the alarm across the room.	E = Forget to set it.
or	*or*
Have parents wake me.	Parents refuse.
or	*or*
Have a friend call.	The friend oversleeps.
or	*or*
Go to bed earlier.	And miss Letterman?

S = Okay, I'll try to go to bed earlier and set the alarm.
P = I'll go to bed by midnight, set the alarm for seven, set it loud, if I don't get up I realize I'll get another detention and I won't ask you to drive me, but if you got me a car then I wouldn't ask you and I'd always be on time.
N = We'll try it and see.

Problem-solve your way through this with flexibility, creativity, and persistence. It's worth it, and you will see that as your stress decreases, things will go more smoothly. Even Einstein knew that!

Index

■   ■   ■

Parenting
disagreement about, 223–25
goals of, 57
sources of ideas about, 32–33
Patience, 77–78, 79, 82, 141, 162,
177, 194, 224
Peer culture, 12–13, 61, 72, 105,
200–206, 212, 214
Perfection, 60, 128–29
Persistence, 29, 77–78, 79, 141,
175, 239
Planning, 15–16, 138–39, 142,
157. *See also* FIG TESPN;
specific topic
Practice, 138–39, 142–43, 205,
222, 223
Praise, 20, 31, 137, 164, 216, 231,
238
and discipline, 84–90, 93, 103
Preschool years, 192–200
Priorities, 90, 135, 216
Problem solving, 17
and anticipating obstacles,
138–39, 142, 225
and commitment, 139, 143
and consequences of actions,
136–37
and follow-up, 139–40, 143
and goals, 134–35, 142
and identification of problem,
133–34, 142
and options, 135–36, 142
and planning, 138–39, 142, 155,
157
questions about, 156–57
and role playing, 138–39,
142–43
and best solution, 137–38,
143
and values, 61–62

See also FIG TESPN; Keep Calm;
Thinking; Trouble Trackers;
specific problem
Progress reports, 183–85
Prompts and education problems,
163–64, 182, 183–84
about feelings, 111, 116–17,
131, 132–33, 156, 163–64
and FIG TESPN, 131, 132–33,
156
and impulse, 111, 116–17
and thinking, 65–68, 72
Punishment, 83, 98, 100, 101, 124,
231

Questioning, 158, 218–19
and FIG TESPN, 128, 133–34,
141–43, 156–57
and hard-to-reach children, 199,
209
techniques of, 60, 62, 70–76
See also specific technique or topic

Reading, 192–93, 198–99
Resistant children, 76, 136,
228–29. *See also* Hard-to-reach
children
Respect, 83, 209, 210, 225, 231,
232
Rewards, 96–97, 208, 209
Road map, 31–39
Role playing, 139, 142–43, 152,
182, 205

Sadness, 235–37
Scoffing by children, 29–31
Self-awareness, 10–11, 83, 90–93,
105–6, 107–11
Self-control, 22–23, 64, 68
and anger, 222, 223

Maurice J. Elias, Ph.D., is a Professor of Psychology at Rutgers University, a member of the Leadership Team of the Collaborative for the Advancement of Social and Emotional Learning, a nationally recognized expert on child and parental problem-solving, and a writer and contributor to numerous professional publications as well as magazine and newspaper articles.

Steven E. Tobias, Psy.D., is director of the Center for Child and Family Development in Morristown, New Jersey. He is an expert on issues of child development, social skills, and Attention-Deficit/Hyperactivity Disorder. He consults to schools and conducts workshops for parents.

Brian S. Friedlander, Ph.D., is a software developer and school psychologist and has a private practice in Long Valley, in New Jersey. His *Interactive Course in Social Problem Solving, Student Conflict Manager*, and *Discipline Tracker* software programs have helped numerous students and educators, as will his forthcoming book, *Computers in Child Therapy*.

The authors can be contacted by E-mail at: www.EQParenting.com.